KENNEDY
AND
JOHNSON

By the same author

MY TWELVE YEARS WITH JOHN F. KENNEDY

KENNEDY AND JOHNSON

BY

EVELYN LINCOLN

HOLT, RINEHART AND WINSTON

NEW YORK CHICAGO SAN FRANCISCO

Published simultaneously in Canada by Holt, Rinehart
and Winston of Canada, Limited.

Library of Congress Catalog Card Number: 68-14927

Published, March, 1968
Fourth Printing, May, 1968

DESIGNER: VINCENT TORRE
8697203
Printed in the United States of America

IN LOVING MEMORY

OF MY FATHER

J. N. NORTON

CONTENTS

Prologue

SINCE 1965, when my first book, *My Twelve Years With John F. Kennedy,* was published, I have been traveling around the country speaking about my experiences as personal secretary to Mr. Kennedy.

Wherever I have gone, from the very beginning, audiences have asked me the same questions over and over again, and in recent days, with more urgency and concern. "What was the relationship," they all ask, "between Kennedy and Johnson?" "What did Mr. Kennedy think of his Vice President?" "How much did Mr. Johnson know of what was going on?" "Did they get along?"

I did not, in my first book, speak a great deal about such matters, trying instead to concentrate on President Kennedy and on my own life with him. However, I have now decided to write about what I saw of the relationship between Mr. Kennedy and Mr. Johnson because so many people seem to want to know, and certainly they deserve whatever information is available.

I do not have the qualifications of a professional historian nor do I, in any way, intend to write a scholarly or definitive history. This book is simply the record of my own observations of the two men during the time I was with them. It is, to the best of my ability, an objective account. Of course, I cannot, nor would I, deny my enormous admiration for John F. Kennedy, nor my personal sadness at his death, but I have tried to record whatever information I have as simply and unemotionally as possible.

From the fall of 1955, I kept a daily diary and careful notes of everything that happened in Mr. Kennedy's office or, if we were traveling, of the events of the trip itself. I would record all visits, all speeches, all schedules, and all the details that occupied each day.

As a matter of fact, Mr. Kennedy had noticed what I was doing and asked me whether I was "planning to write a book." I told him that I had no such idea, but that I thought *he* might someday want to write his memoirs, and, in that case, would find a daily diary useful.

In addition, I was in an especially good position to act as a "sieve" for all information coming into the office. Reporters, staff members, visitors, members of the family would all stop by my desk and keep me "up to the minute" on whatever we were then involved in. Reports, minutes of meetings, letters and memoranda would, of course, pass across my desk, and I made note of them in my diary.

I have used my diary and all these other sources in writing this book, and I hope that the result will give, to those who are interested, some new insights into one of the most crucial—and painful—periods in American history.

EVELYN LINCOLN

Washington, D.C.
November, 1967

KENNEDY AND JOHNSON

CHAPTER

I

Two Men

"WE ARE LOOKING FORWARD to a new life and a new baby." With this rare political reference to his personal life, the man who was soon to become the thirty-fifth President of the United States prepared to leave damp and chilly Hyannis Port, Massachusetts for the sun and sea of southern Florida. He had gone there when he was recuperating from the spinal operation that almost killed him, and he was going there now to recuperate from the aching fatigue of an exhausting election campaign.

But he knew that the number of lazy days he would spend at his father's Palm Beach home was limited. There was a Cabinet to build, strategy to plan, issues to clarify. And then there was the job of getting to know that man, Lyndon Johnson, who was the only other American elected to a political office by the votes of all the people. Of course, he had known Mr. Johnson from working with him in the Senate. But their relationship, which never had been close, often had been cool and, at times, had been deeply hostile, was now one of partnership. It was almost as if Romeo and Juliet had gotten married, and now Mr. Montague must somehow try to get along with Mr. Capulet.

Actually, the difference between John Fitzgerald Kennedy, Irish Catholic New Englander, and Lyndon Baines Johnson, white Anglo-Saxon Protestant Southwesterner, was far more basic than that between a Montague and a Capulet. After all, these feuding families both lived in Verona. John Kennedy and Lyndon Johnson lived in different worlds.

This would have made their relationship difficult enough, but magnifying every difference in viewpoint, multiplying every little irritation and friction, was the fact that they were both strong, proud, and possessed of a keen sense of their own worth and importance. Never in my lifetime had I seen two more determined men occupying the chief office of the land.

On the surface, of course, it was necessary that they show a smooth and even relationship. But underneath—behind the scenes—there was a smoldering irritability.

A great many Americans had paid little attention to John Kennedy while he was a Senator. But, perhaps because we all wanted a change after the Eisenhower doldrums, and perhaps also because his staff was so good at image-making, newspapers and magazines began to wonder if perhaps the Kennedy victory might be more important than the usual outcome of a political contest. He seemed so keen and thoughtful and well-educated. Perhaps his election might mean victory for an intellectual style in American politics. Perhaps, from now on, they wrote, it will seem natural, even expected, for a Presidential candidate to have credentials that include a fine education, travel, authorship. Certainly many of these columnists and writers, whether they were right or wrong, thought they saw in John Kennedy a kindred spirit, another intellectual.

Lyndon Johnson, on the other hand, was a Last Frontiersman on the New Frontier. He seemed out of place and out of step with the tone set by the new Administration. But one thing was certain: he would never be out of sight, as so many of his predecessors in the Vice Presidency had been.

A few days after Mr. Kennedy arrived in Palm Beach, he decided to give up the dream of a restful vacation. He turned his father's home into his base of operations until the Inauguration. He asked me to come down from Washington and join him there.

During the time I was at Palm Beach, Lyndon Johnson visited Mr. Kennedy three times. His first visit was to report on what he had learned as Mr. Kennedy's special representative at the NATO Parliamentarian's Conference in Paris. He arrived on a glorious day, the sun and soft breezes straight out of a Florida tourist brochure. The sun was reflected softly from the stately, white Kennedy home, and in the background was the soft rumble and hiss of waves gently falling against the beach. The President-elect was reading reports and papers in one of his favorite spots—out by the swimming pool which was shaded by palm trees swaying and rustling in the light wind.

On his way to the pool Mr. Kennedy had asked me to alert him shortly before the arrival of Mr. Johnson. "I want to have a chance to change my clothes," he said. I suppose he didn't want to appear before his Vice President dressed in lounging clothes. I did alert him, and it wasn't long thereafter that a Secret Service agent called me, saying, "Mrs. Lincoln, Mr. Johnson is on his way." A few seconds later he appeared at the entryway of the patio.

I had seen Lyndon Johnson many times, but since this was the first time I had seen him since the election I watched him closely as he walked across the patio. The primary impression was one of heaviness. Heavy footsteps. Heavy body. Heavy, slow-moving motions. He walked strangely, with his body bent slightly to the right, his shoulders and arms moving around as though they were paddling him forward.

"Good morning, Senator," I said as I held the door open for him. He nodded his greeting and then stood in the hallway looking both ways. As I relieved him of his wide-brimmed hat I told him, "If you will have a seat in the living room, Mr. Kennedy will join you very, very soon." I left him standing there while I was off across the room to tell Mr. Kennedy that Mr. Johnson had arrived. I noticed that Mr. Johnson was studying the dining room to his left with its long massive table and chairs. That table had a history in itself, because it was around its sides that first Joe, Jr., then John, Bob, Ted, and the girls had gathered for long discussions about politics or their experiences at school or during their travels.

The living room in which Senator Johnson was asked to wait was beautifully decorated. There were pictures of the Kennedy family and grandchildren on the walls and on the baby grand piano over in the corner. Comfortable sofas and chairs were tastefully placed throughout. Mr. Johnson sat down near the center of the room, from where he could look out the wide windows over the ocean to the end of the sky.

It wasn't long before Mr. Kennedy came out of his bedroom. He brushed his hair off his forehead, walked swiftly and lightly toward Mr. Johnson, greeting him with a smile, "Hello there, Lyndon. Did you have a nice trip?" He held out his hand. As he did, Mr. Johnson, his head tilted to the left, pushed himself out of his chair and grabbed at the outstretched hand, saying, "H'ya Jack." Then they sat down to talk things over.

Several times during their conversation I took telephone messages into Mr. Kennedy. Each time I noticed that Mr. Johnson was slumping farther and farther down in his chair. The 225 pounds seemed to spill over. He was a vigorous talker, frowning and pointing a forefinger toward Mr. Kennedy to accentuate his statements. The President-elect listened intently, said very little and, to someone who didn't know him, would have appeared relaxed. But while Mr. Johnson talked, Mr. Kennedy's right foot was continually twitching, and his fingers made a rat-ta-tat noise on the arm of his chair.

After about an hour or so of serious discussion about plans for the Administration, Mr. Kennedy asked Mr. Johnson if he would like to take a dip before lunch. Mr. Johnson accepted and before too long they were drifting out of the room to dress for the pool.

I guess water is not the natural element for anyone who grew up on parched earth, for the tall Texan seemed to be increasingly uncomfortable. He hesitated on the edge of the pool every time before plunging in. When he came up for air, he looked around unhappily, and seemed greatly relieved when I came out to tell them that lunch would be ready shortly.

Bits and pieces of the conversation floated in to me through the door of my little office as the two men sat out on the patio having a lunch of melon and baked chicken with string beans and potatoes. There didn't seem to be any great disagreement between them. The only difference seemed to be in their voices. At times Mr. Johnson's voice came through a little louder.

The men stood up. It was time for Mr. Johnson to leave. "Mrs. Lincoln," Mr. Kennedy called, "will you bring Lyndon's hat. He is leaving."

They shook hands. And their first meeting since the election was over.

A few weeks later Mr. Johnson came again, but this time he was not alone. With him was his old friend and sponsor, Speaker Sam Rayburn of Texas. What an uneven looking pair they were as they rounded the bend to enter the patio. They were both stockily built, but Mr. Johnson towered over the Speaker. "Mr. Sam," as he was called by his colleagues, looked as weathered as a rock that had been battered by many a storm, and I suppose being leader in the House of Representatives is equivalent to bearing up under a lifetime of storms. As they entered, I could see Mr. Johnson had modified his style slightly. Though he still talked and gestured in non-stop fashion to Mr. Sam, there was an element of courtship there. He was plainly trying his best to please the older man. During their walk Mr. Sam grunted a few times, but otherwise said nothing.

Once again I was the one who opened the door and as I took their wide-brimmed hats I was immediately conscious of how much Mr. Sam had aged. His normally deep voice seemed shaky, and he tottered slightly as he walked ahead of Mr. Johnson into the living room.

Mr. Johnson must have been accustomed to early

rising because when I came back from my hotel to the Kennedy house the next morning, he was already awake. He sat at the far end of the dining-room table, in his silk bathrobe with its LBJ monogram, slumped over and staring into space. The cook told me that she was fixing his breakfast, and that it would be ready shortly. As I passed into my office, a few steps away, I assured him that his breakfast was on its way. I had noticed that Mr. Johnson had pulled the *New York Times* out of the neatly arranged pile of papers at the head of the table near Mr. Kennedy's place setting. I wondered how Mr. Kennedy would react to this when he came out for breakfast. His favorite morning reading would be missing. I was sorry that I didn't have another copy.

"Good morning, Lyndon, you're up early this morning," said Mr. Kennedy, somewhat sleepily. "Good morning, Jack," he replied. "You like to get up early, too." Mr. Kennedy, who had also come out into the dining room in his terry-cloth bathrobe, was ready for breakfast. He fingered through the papers—looking for the *New York Times.* He started to call me but then he said "Never mind," for he had noticed the paper he wanted—lying untouched by the side of Mr. Johnson's plate. Mr. Johnson couldn't, of course, know how important it was to Mr. Kennedy to read the papers the very first thing in the morning, especially the *New York Times.* Instead, he started to talk in his usual energetic manner. Mr. Kennedy said nothing, but I knew from certain little signs, that he was terribly upset. When I went into the room with a telephone message, he hardly acknowledged it. He sipped at his orange juice, fingered the papers once again, then stood up, excused himself, and stalked back through the living room on his way to his bedroom. As he reached the bedroom door, he shouted out to me, "Bring me a cup of coffee."

When I entered his bedroom, he was standing at the window staring at the dark, misty, gloomy day outside. "What gall," he said. "If he had the paper why didn't he read it? Or at least give someone else a chance to see it." With that he shook off his irritation. "I will be out shortly. I am going to dress. Get Pierre on the phone," he said, and I quickly called Pierre Salinger.

Mr. Johnson must have gone up to his bedroom to dress, because the dining room was now empty. However, the paper still lay untouched on the table. I hurriedly picked it up and rushed to Mr. Kennedy's bedroom. He was delighted to see it.

On this trip, Florida was not smiling at Lyndon Johnson. Instead of warm sun and soft breezes, there were threatening rain clouds overhead, a brisk wind laced with fine rain and mist in the air. However, Speaker Rayburn didn't seem to mind, because shortly after breakfast, he put on an old gray raincoat and rain hat and took a stroll around the grounds. He ended up by standing out by the sea wall with one of the groundkeepers, casting for fish.

The other two men were cooped up in the house where they seemed to be playing musical chairs. Every time I walked into the room they had changed places or were sitting in some new spot in the room. And every time I entered with a telephone message they both looked up eagerly, expectantly—as though they were waiting for some earth-shaking announcement.

Later on in the day, Senator Mike Mansfield of Montana, the anticipated successor to Majority Leader Johnson, came out to the house. Senator Mansfield was a quiet soft-speaking man whose personal style was certainly in contrast to what Senator Johnson had brought to the Senate post. The four men huddled together in the living room discussing the legislative course to be taken during the next session of Congress. Mr. Johnson did most of the talking, Mr. Kennedy did most of the listening, and there were side remarks by Speaker Rayburn. I am sure they were hoping that the legislative program they were working on would be somewhat more brilliant than the lackluster lame duck congressional session they had returned to after the convention.

When Mr. Johnson next visited Palm Beach he brought with him, unannounced, his wife Lady Bird, Congressman and Mrs. Mendel Rivers of South Carolina, and Congressman and Mrs. Frank Boykin of Alabama.

When a member of Mr. Johnson's staff called to tell me that these people were on their way with Mr. Johnson, I dashed through the dining room and into the living room to tell Mr. Kennedy the news. "My God," said Mr. Kennedy, "there is only one thing to do and that is to fix my bedroom here on the first floor for Senator and Mrs. Johnson. Move my things up to Dad's bedroom on the second floor, and then invite them all out to the house for lunch today."

The weather was playing tricks again. It was much too breezy on the patio for the luncheon. A better place was the somewhat sheltered area on the ocean side of the house, even though the tablecloth whipped in the wind.

There was much good-natured talk and laughter as this group appeared on the patio. It was a get-together certainly with a decidedly southern atmosphere. I could see that Mr. Johnson was in an especially good mood. He was carrying on a conversation with flamboyant Congressman Boykin, whose campaign theme was "Everything is made for love." Congressman Rivers, a ranking member of the House Armed Services Committee, a man with neatly combed gray hair, was quietly following along, while the women faded into the background. As I let them into the hall, there were shouts of, "Hi ya, Jack." "You remember Bird." "Oh, certainly." "Hello, Congressman . . ." The chattering continued as Mr. Kennedy escorted them into the living room for a little relaxation before lunch. Mr. Kennedy's mother, who was in Palm Beach at the time, also joined the group.

All during lunch, Mr. Johnson carried the conversation though Congressman Rivers chimed in now and then. His chief interest seemed to be the Charleston Naval Base, located in his district. He was upset that President Eisenhower had not done more for the base, and he hoped that the new Administration would give it more attention. Congressman Boykin had all kinds of patronage problems that he wanted Mr. Kennedy to know about.

In spite of the weather, by then the wind had picked up and rain seemed likely, and the confusion before the luncheon, all ended rather peacefully.

The next morning the squall was all over, the guests had departed, and the household settled down to normal. Mr. Kennedy asked me to tell the housekeeper, the cook, and the others how much he appreciated their very fine handling of a very awkward situation.

Just four days after he had arrived in Palm Beach for a rest, and eight days after the election, Mr. Kennedy was off to the LBJ Ranch. Possibly for moral support, he took with him his house guest and former Harvard roommate, Congressman Torbert Macdonald. When they returned back the next evening both were exhausted. "We'll fill you in tomorrow," Torb said, "but right now we need some sleep."

I couldn't wait to hear all about the trip the next morning. Down in the coffee shop in the hotel where I was staying, newspapermen gave me sketches of some of the things that took place, but I was more anxious to talk to Mr. Kennedy and "Torb"—to learn their reactions of Texas, the LBJ Ranch, and how Mr. Johnson acted in his native habitat.

Of course, Mr. Kennedy had been to Texas before, not only during the campaign, but on other occasions. He had campaigned in Texas during the 1956 Presidential election, traveling to El Paso, Laredo, San Antonio—with a visit to the Alamo and ending up by attending a breakfast held at the airport in Dallas. Therefore, he was familiar with the vast scenes and wide open spaces—the long stretches of emptiness and almost featureless small hills, where, once in a while one would see a pecan or a cypress tree.

I, too, had been to Texas many times and found it much like the description Mr. Sam had once given. "I was raised on a poor back country Texas farm. As a young boy, on Sunday I would sit on the fence and just wish to God that somebody would ride by on a horse or drive past in a buggy—anything that would relieve my loneliness."

Some of this territory was so hard to live in that there was nothing to do but to joke about it. In dry, windy Amarillo, they say, if your hat blows off you just reach up and pull down another one.

And a stranger once asked a Texan, "Does the wind always blow this way?" "Oh, no, sometimes it blows the other way," he answered.

I think that the harsh conditions and loneliness helped to create in certain leaders, such as Mr. Sam and Lyndon Johnson, a genuine concern for others. But the limitless horizon and more than human scale seemed also to create, in some, a ruthless self-seeking. A colorful "jes plain folks" kind of politicking was prevalent in these vast areas and had been known to produce men of common manners, but uncommon achievement; but it had also produced self-centered buffoons and phonies. It has been said that this is what makes Texas politics so interesting and mysterious—the problems of sorting out the types, the genuine from the phonies. Obviously, this is not an easy task for non-Texans.

I learned from the conversation with Congressman Macdonald of Massachusetts at breakfast next morning that it was cloudy and misty as the Kennedy party landed at the airstrip on the LBJ Ranch. When the door of the plane opened, they saw Mr. Johnson in an open-throated cream-colored leather jacket, ranch pants, cowboy boots, and ten-gallon hat loping toward them. He was in extremely high spirits. He was waving and shouting. "Did you notice he didn't even remove that hat until I made a remark about it," Mr. Kennedy said, "and then how upset he got when I didn't want my picture taken with that hat on my head. It took a little time for him to understand why I would rather not do it. I guess they did take a picture of me holding it in my hand."

Then Congressman Macdonald and the press staff members went on to describe how Mr. Johnson took them on a tour of the old home place in an open white convertible—even though it was raining. Out there in the West they had learned to live with the weather, so what was a little rain? It would have to hail before a Texan would run for the barn.

Everyone who visits the LBJ Ranch is forewarned that Lyndon B. Johnson, in true Texas style, is extremely proud of his wife, proud of his daughters, proud of his ancestors, proud of his ranch, proud of his cattle, and proud of his state. On the flag pole in front of his ranch house are three flags: the flag of the United States, the flag of Texas, and the personal flag of LBJ—white letters on a blue background. Everything is bigger and better in Texas, and Texans, someone has said, are so happy about their Lone Star State they can't sleep at night.

Mr. Kennedy and Torb described how Mr. Johnson drove the car, and as they took the bumpy tour pointed out the sights. Every once in a while, he would shout messages over the car's radiophone to the ranch house. It seemed that he was in control of every detail and that nothing happened on the ranch unless he approved. At one time he blared out, "We're down here by Grandpap's house, near the old graveyard."

As they rode along, Mr. Kennedy and Mr. Johnson had many events to talk about. Texans were still talking about how the young Massachusetts Catholic only two months before had taken on and won over a bristling crowd of Protestant Texas ministers at the Rice

Hotel in Houston. They also discussed the campaign and the election. But the most serious matter to discuss was Mr. Kennedy's desire that Mr. Johnson attend the inter-parliamentary foreign ministers conference in Europe as his representative.

After the tour, Mr. Johnson drove them back to the ranch house and to a treatment of real southern hospitality. It was common knowledge that the LBJ was famous for political and social gatherings. The barbecue pit sizzled with spareribs, thick steaks, or chicken. The cooks were so busy they hardly had time to wipe smoke tears from their eyes. And guests were from everywhere—literally—for at times the airstrip, filled with private planes, resembled a crowded parking lot in the heart of any large city.

There were always gifts for the guests with a flavor of Texas and the LBJ Ranch. There might be ashtrays decorated with the map of the ranch, dishes with historic Texas events baked upon them, or a box of cookies, each cut in the shape of Texas. Mr. Johnson had talked about these cookies in his campaign talks. For the children, what could be better than a cowboy suit? But the favorite gift for any visiting dignitary was a ten-gallon Stetson hat, a mark of distinction in Texas.

I could tell from the tone of the conversation at the breakfast table that Mr. Kennedy and Torb both had been ill-at-ease in this confused environment, particularly since the motto seemed to be that "noise is golden." There were loudspeakers all over the ranch. These horns reached out to the swimming pool and the celebrated old oak tree near the ranch house, to the guest house, on to the foreman's house and even out in the corrals. When the system was not being used to relay orders, Muzak from the Johnson radio station in Austin came over the wires.

Mr. Johnson especially liked to recall that he was not always used to such luxuries. He enjoyed telling how as a boy he had pushed the soil of Texas through his toes; or how as a little shaver he stood barefooted by the side of his father's desk in the state legislature in Austin listening to Texas politicians "wheeling and dealing." "I have worked all my life," the newspaper reports him as saying. "As a little boy I shined shoes at the barbershop; as a printer's devil I worked on the paper on Thursday afternoon, the old Press. When I graduated from High School at fifteen, I wanted a job but there were no jobs to be found around here in 1924. So I took this fellow's advice and went West young man, worked two years in California—finally I wound up in a lawyer's office."

Mr. Johnson continued to describe this period in his life. "I came back home and mother talked me into going to college, and during the period I was in college I taught school down in south Texas. It gave me great satisfaction; I thought I wanted to be a teacher. When I finished college, I went to Houston and taught a year, and then a great opportunity in my life came to me when Congressman Kleberg, one of the owners of the King Ranch, asked me to go to Washington as his secretary in the Hoover Administration in 1931, and except for a brief period of fifteen months I have been in Washington ever since—twelve years in the House, twelve years in the Senate, five years as Majority Leader."

Occasionally he would get off a joke on himself. He was not born at the present big ranch house, he explained. "I was born down the road about half a mile. One of my friends observed the other day that I had gone a long way in the world. I had moved up the river about four hundred yards!"

It seems that Mr. Johnson also had his light side. He was a great mimic and loved to poke fun at some of the politicians he had worked with. So, on that trip, while they were waiting for supper, he entertained them with political stories and mimics. This they enjoyed, and they also enjoyed a delicious charcoal broiled steak dinner. Then there were more stories of the Wild West days. Finally, Mr. Kennedy decided that it was time to go to bed, especially after learning that they were all getting up at 6:00 in the morning to hunt deer.

The confusion the night before was nothing compared to the confusion that prevailed in the morning. I could easily imagine Mr. Kennedy, up too early, poking at his venison sausage and squirming at the thought of the six hours ahead.

According to Torb Macdonald and Mr. Kennedy, Johnson was in his element. He was blasting orders over the loudspeakers to the cowhands and to the people in the house—and those orders were obeyed. People kept popping in and out of doors as though they were chasing each other.

Soon it was time for the hunt to begin. They lined up all the cars with Mr. Johnson's convertible in the lead. "Come along, Jack," Mr. Johnson called, and as soon as Mr. Kennedy climbed into the car with him they were off for the chase. They rode and rode over the ranch, out to the foothills. "I see something moving over there in the bushes," someone said. Then Mr. Kennedy said a gun was thrust into his hands and before he knew what had happened they all shouted, "Ya got him. Ya got him." "If I got him I certainly didn't aim," said Mr. Kennedy, "but there on the ground lay that dead deer."

The hunt continued for several more hours, and I guess there were others who shot and killed deer, but I am sure that Mr. Kennedy was greatly relieved when the thundering herd of hunters returned to the ranch house. He didn't especially care for this type of sport, especially not at 6:00 in the morning.

I heard more about the trip during lunch and out near the pool. I also read the public statement that Mr. Kennedy released before he left the LBJ Ranch, honoring his host who had worked hard for him in the campaign and with whom he was to face an uncertain future. "It is my belief," he had said, "that Senator Johnson's great talents and experience equip him to be the most effective Vice President in our history."

At the hotel that evening reporters filled me in with a further description of the LBJ Ranch. They said that their gracious hostess, Lady Bird, took the reporters who accompanied Mr. Kennedy on a tour in the Johnson tour bus. She sat at a microphone describing the various landmarks. The LBJ tours were a standard procedure, although they varied to the time allowed and, of course, the season. Sometimes there were flash floods, or the Pedernales River would overflow, and then in the summer there was that merciless sun. But this was November, so they were given a fairly long tour.

Always included among the sights was the century-old oak tree, then out to the corrals where the ranch hands worked with the horses. As the bus rolled along, calves bawled and off in the distance were the pride of the ranch, the handsome white-faced Herefords. There was also a buffalo roaming the grass land to give a touch of the past. Also it seemed always to be assumed that guests were eager to see the Johnson cemetery.

The tour was never completely over until the guests traveled to the little school house where Mr. Johnson went to school. Then, they drove along buck bushes and bull nettles and long bare patches of the road to Johnson City for a tour of the famed cottage on 9th Street where Lyndon Johnson lived as a boy.

There was not much to see in Johnson City, just the Pilgrim's Restaurant, Roy's Drive In and Furr's Cafe, the home of the Furrburger. Reporters told me it was also known for other attractions—potlicker, cracklin' bread, and fried jack rabbit. It was also the country that seemed to produce the largest crop of Burma Shave signs—an echo of the past. The whole area seemed to them full of such echoes.

The tour group headed back toward the ranch, but no matter how fatigued, they learned that all visitors to LBJ country paid a visit to the small cottage of Lyndon Johnson's gray-haired cousin Oriole. Oriole's politics were simple. She loved to talk about Franklin D. Roosevelt and Lyndon Johnson, and on the wall of her home was a campaign poster she had saved from his earliest campaign—the poster read, "Roosevelt and Unity." While Oriole's politics were simple, her religion was not. She was a "Christodelphian" and the visitors were still pondering what a Christodelphian was as they drove back to the ranch house.

Texas politics was also something worth pondering. Did you ever hear of Governor Jim Hogg of Texas who campaigned with his daughter, Ima? Sure, was the reply, and he was the best governor Texas has had in modern times. Mr. Johnson had at one time presented a biography of Governor Hogg to Mr. Kennedy and when the Johnsons stayed overnight in Austin, they usually stayed in the Jim Hogg suite in the Driskill Hotel.

In a roughneck way, they said, Jim Hogg appealed to ranch hands and dirt farmers. He would tell them:

"I may not make 45 in English grammar
I may not make 55 in History, but I'll
make a grade of 75,000 majority in the election!"

Hogg's approach apparently worked.

Of course, this "jes plain folks" approach to politics was not only confined to Texas. Massachusetts had one of its own in Mayor James Curley, and, in fact, in the President-elect's favorite grandfather, "Honey Fitz." Mr. Kennedy also had emerged from this sort of politics.

Mr. Johnson, the politician, could only be understood in the light of the kind of politics he faced and surmounted as he grew into national prominence. The two bigger-than-life people who had backed the candidates Mr. Johnson had fought in his first races for the United States Senate were "Ma" and "Pa" Ferguson, both Governors of Texas at one time or another. Ferguson told his chew-and-spit crowds, "You have only three friends in the world. God Almighty, Sears Roebuck and Jim Ferguson."

Governor James E. "Pa" Ferguson, after his folksy campaign, was impeached for shady financial dealings. He was dubbed as a "man with hayseed in his hair and a bankroll in his hand." Mr. Kennedy once wrote that this type of a politician makes "the poor think he is a friend of the poor—the rich know he is not."

When Pa Ferguson's impeachment provided that he could never serve in public office in Texas again, he had his wife run for Governor and she won. Governor Miriam "Ma" Ferguson served as a front for her husband. Among her other activities, she issued 2,000 pardons during her first twenty months in office. After her first term she unsuccessfully ran four more times —her husband was still technically barred—and she finally won again in the early thirties.

Ma and Pa Ferguson remained a force to back Lyndon Johnson's rivals for the United States Senate: W. Lee O'Daniel, who beat Mr. Johnson in 1941 by a few hotly disputed votes; and Coke Stevenson in 1948 when Mr. Johnson won by 87 hotly disputed votes. These races were somewhat different than running against Henry Cabot Lodge for the Senate as Mr. Kennedy had done.

Mr. Johnson's first race for the United States Senate was so colorful that Texans have never forgotten it. None who witnessed it could possibly have been surprised later at the Texan's later antics.

The stage for this first Senate race of Lyndon Johnson was set by the chief contender, Governor W. Lee "Pappy" O'Daniel. When a Texas Senator died, Governor O'Daniel filled the Senate vacancy in a way that made it possible for him to serve as Governor for a while longer, but to insure the Senate seat for himself. What he did was to appoint the eighty-seven-year-old son of the Texas hero, Sam Houston. Who could object to this? Aside from his historical credentials, Texas was supposed to respect age. Mr. Houston lived up to expectations by dying quickly after being sworn in, and O'Daniel immediately said he himself would run to take the old gentleman's seat. So did Congressman Lyndon Johnson from the district around Austin.

In that Democratic primary, candidates ran with backgrounds ranging from chiropractor to plumber. Most colorful of all was "Goat Gland" Brinkley of Del Rio, Texas, who safely broadcast advertisements for his youth restoring goat glands from across the Mexican border. There were also several other Bible Belt politicians Texas called "calamity howlers."

Pappy O'Daniel and Lyndon Johnson could not compete with "Goat Gland" Brinkley for color, but they put on a pretty good show anyway. Pappy, a former flour salesman and Texas editor, radio broadcaster, and composer was one of the best vote-getters Texas ever saw. He got his nickname from one of his songs, "Pass the Biscuits Pappy." With an eye to the mother vote, Pappy would boom out from his radio program with, "Hello there, mother, beautiful sweetheart. How in the world are you anyway, you little bunch of sweetness? This is your big boy, W. Lee O'Daniel." Mr. Johnson's opponent then might swing into a rendition of his own composition, "The Boy Who Never Grew Too Old to Comb His Mother's Hair," followed by "Beautiful, Beautiful Texas." When Pappy took to the campaign trail, he took along an extra crooner named Texas Rose. In the tradition of

Governor Hogg introducing his daughter Ima, Pappy would introduce his three children, Patty Boy, Mickey Wicky, and Molly.

Pappy denounced the "gang of back-slapping, pie-eating, pussy-footing professional politicians" around Roosevelt "who couldn't run a peanut stand." He scorned the tales of grandeur Congressman Lyndon Johnson brought back from Washington. "That boy," O'Daniel scoffed, "says he's so friendly with the President he can just walk right in the White House and fry his eggs on the White House stove."

Candidate Johnson was not to be outdone. He couldn't sing himself, but he brought to his big rallies a huge lady singer called the Kate Smith of the South. Also warming up the speaking was a large troop including a swing band, tap dancers, and acrobats. To hold the people to the end Mr. Johnson would have a lottery—the lucky number winning a defense bond. "Is there a big crowd?" Johnson would ask then, just as he did in his later years.

Patriotism was Johnson's first line of approach in his speeches. The way to be against Hitler, he said, was to vote for Johnson. Everybody must "line up in unity behind the Commander-in-chief." Pappy O'Daniel's approach was more basic. He made the Ten Commandments the heart of his program. Lyndon Johnson, likewise, quoted the Bible and intoned "come let us reason together." This was followed by a lot of "turnip green" talk.

"Pass the Biscuits Pappy" won this race by slightly more than 1,000 votes. Mr. Johnson had to wait for another time to make his move to the Senate.

Everyone on that trip to the LBJ Ranch knew that Mr. Johnson and Mr. Kennedy lived in two different universes and that any future cooperation was uncertain. There was harmony on the surface between the two leaders, but the bad blood from their recent campaign encounters was hard to forget and sure to remain in American politics for years to come.

Some said the difference between the two men was just the difference of style and that it didn't affect the way the two men would run a government. Others said there would be the difference of night and day between their conduct of office.

Who was right? It was fascinating, there was no doubt about that. Perhaps the difference between them is best summed up in the telegram sent by the Vice-President elect to Mr. Kennedy when the Kennedy baby was born: "Name that boy Lyndon Johnson and a heifer calf will be his."

CHAPTER

II

The Early Primary Race

POLITICAL BATTLES shape up in strange ways. Sometimes men who might have gone their separate ways never entangling their lives and fortunes, but never conflicting either, find themselves in bitter combat simply because their political stars are in the ascendancy at the same time.

Mr. Kennedy's political fortune was rising rapidly. He felt he must try for the big prize in 1960 or he might not make it at all later on. If he was passed over in 1960, it would be said he was passed over because of his religion, and then it might be a long time before his party would consider giving the nomination to a non-Protestant nominee. Mr. Kennedy would not step aside, and he was not interested—and made it very plain that he was not interested—in becoming the Vice-Presidential nominee.

It was also a crucial year for Majority Leader Johnson. He was at the peak of his power in the Senate, and it seemed unlikely that he would be able to increase this power, particularly if a Democrat were elected President. Signals would then be called from the Oval Room of the White House and not the Majority Leader's palatial office. Also, he could not be certain that in the forthcoming Presidential year he would be able to keep control of his unruly Texas delegation. Many of Mr. Johnson's Texas Democrats did not appreciate his attempts at being a national politician rather than just a southern politician. As he said when he returned from a Texas political brawl, it was getting harder for him to hold his political buggy in the road. Therefore, if the tall Texan did not make the big try in 1960 he might find his star wavering and his support drifting away.

Mr. Johnson, like Mr. Kennedy, was championing a minority cause. Mr. Johnson felt that if he couldn't get the nomination with his great record it would be only because he was from a minority, a Southerner, and it would be a long time before another Southerner would have a crack at the White House.

So political fate brought these two strong men into a serious and scarring duel. Because the harshness of the contest was secondary when it was taking place, many were unable to understand some of the political echoes from the conflict which were to affect American politics for years to come.

Exactly what did happen in this political duel between the two talented Senators is worth knowing because it tells a lot about the political character of the two men and sheds light on the question of who was the abler political leader. The political test of strength between Mr. Kennedy and Mr. Johnson began with John Kennedy's failure to win the Vice-Presidential nomination in 1956.

I heard John F. Kennedy say many times, "If I had been chosen as Vice-Presidential nominee at the Democratic Convention in Chicago in 1956, my political career would now be over."

Actually, his try for the second place on the Stevenson ticket couldn't have worked out better if he had planned it with superhuman cunning. As a result of his hard fight for the Vice-Presidential nomination and his photofinish race with Senator Estes Kefauver, the press gave him tremendous coverage. It made him a national figure. Further, since he had come so close to winning it seemed strong evidence that his religion was not an impediment. Also, the way he conducted himself after his convention defeat was extremely appealing. He was not only a good loser, but a graceful loser. He left no doubt that the candidates chosen by the convention would get his wholehearted support. This party loyalty stored up much good will, which he used to keen advantage four years later.

Although I never saw John F. Kennedy lack confidence in himself, the outpouring of letters and telegrams after the convention fed his conviction that he need not fear for his political future. One of the typical letters read, "I cried when you didn't win out. Just wait until I am a little older, I will vote for you to be *President.*" The 1956 Convention was a major crossroad in his career. I knew, of course, that he had for a long time secretly harbored ideas about running for the Presidency, and now I could sense his growing conviction that if he was ever going to be a candidate, it would have to be in 1960.

There were others who had that same feeling about themselves. One was, of course, the Senate Majority Leader, Lyndon B. Johnson. Close behind him were two of his Senate colleagues, Hubert H. Humphrey of Minnesota and Stuart Symington of Missouri. Also, although he had twice failed as the Democratic nominee, and told everyone he was no longer interested, former Illinois Governor Adlai Stevenson could not be discounted. He still had great political appeal to many people.

Actually, the list of possible candidates was unique since, with the exception of Stevenson, all were United States Senators. And they were Senators at a time when the national attention was directed right at Congress. President Eisenhower, though he certainly possessed many fine qualities, was by no means an active or aggressive politician. The initiative, which normally comes from the White House, had been seized by the Congress. The press naturally moves to the source of news, and news came from Congress, not the White House. Lyndon B. Johnson, the shrewd Senate Majority Leader and his close friend and sponsor, Speaker of the House Sam Rayburn, both Texans, were able to keep the focus on themselves, on the Democratic Party, and on Democratic Senators.

Speaker Sam Rayburn had a deep thundering voice that he used to very good advantage in rounding up Democratic votes. When he wanted Democratic members on the floor, he didn't rely on some subordinate to make the calls, he did it himself. And as soon as a Congressman's office heard the telephone operator say, "The Speaker is calling," out came the blast, "Get your member on the floor." Then to the astonishment of the listener, he would hang up. This command proved to be as effective as a high voltage cattle prod in a Texas round-up. The member quickly got out on the floor.

The Majority Leader operated differently. He left the telephone calling to his assistant, Bobby Baker, who in turn would delegate it to others who worked in the Senate Democratic Cloak Room. Mr. Johnson used the telephone sparingly, reserving his calls for special occasions. His voice could be high pitched when he was irritated, or it could be cajoling and soft when he was asking a favor. It depended on what mood he was in, or what he wanted.

One morning in 1957, I handed a letter to Mr. Kennedy and said, "I see you have been chosen as a member of the Senate Foreign Relations Committee this year." The letter was signed by Lyndon Johnson. "Yes, I know, he told me," Mr. Kennedy replied, without raising his head. When the press heard, they made quite an issue over this selection. The Majority Leader had broken a precedent by bypassing lone wolf Senator Kefauver to name Mr. Kennedy to this committee. I thought of what Mr. Kennedy had said about his political career being over if he had been selected as the Vice-Presidential nominee at the convention in Chicago, and I murmured to myself, "That's just what happened to Mr. Kefauver. They no longer feel they need him."

The memos, letters, notes, and telephone calls of the years from 1957 to 1960 leave a clear trail of how Mr. Kennedy was planning his campaign. "The Democratic leadership is dead set against me," I heard him say. "I have only one recourse, and that is to go to the people—enter the primaries—talk to the delegates."

One of the barometers of Senator Kennedy's rising popularity was the number of speaking invitations we received. Hundreds of them, from all parts of the country and many different kinds of groups, poured across my desk but only those were chosen which would not interfere with his work in the Senate, yet would give him exposure in the right places at the right time. In 1959 it was easier for him to determine these choice spots because of the advance men he had carefully placed out in the field, who were constantly taking the political temperature.

Lyndon B. Johnson, on the other hand, stayed close to the Senate since he was bent on making an image of the greatest Majority Leader of all time, and therefore the logical Democratic nominee for the Presidency in 1960. The atmosphere under which he worked was tense and dramatic. Each piece of legislation was discussed, rejected, or passed as though it were a delicate operation that only the chief surgeon, Lyndon Johnson, could perform. He kept the Senate in session night after night. Senators never knew when or where they would be called with an urgent message to rush to the floor. "This vote is important to Democrats. Those who don't vote will find it embarrassing to them later," I was told time and time again by the Democratic cloakroom.

My job was to see that the Senator was on the floor, and so, as soon as I received such a message, the search was on, not in a day, not in an hour, not in five minutes, but NOW, I had to locate him. When I reached Senator Kennedy he'd ask, "Mrs. Lincoln, are you sure that there is going to be a vote?" To this I would answer, "I have checked clear up to Bobby Baker, and he tells me it is a must," "Okay," he would say, "where is Muggsie?" "Right by your front door," I would say. Every Congressman is allotted some job according to seniority, such as policeman or guard or perhaps postal clerk. Then, the

Congressman can bring a young man from his own state who perhaps wants to attend school at night or have the opportunity of living in Washington.

John J. "Muggsie" O'Leary was a young man to whom Mr. Kennedy had given such a job. He was a policeman in the Senate who, after Senate hours, always stood ready to drive Mr. Kennedy wherever he wanted to go. All this pressure to appear on the Senate floor often did end in a roll call vote; but there were also many, many times when it didn't. "What time did you leave the floor, Mr. Kennedy?" I would ask on the morning after one of those pressure sessions. "Oh, around two thirty A.M. I guess," he would reply, "and they never did vote."

The big day arrived: January 2, 1960. This was the day that Mr. Kennedy was going to announce his candidacy for the Democratic nomination for the Presidency. It was 12:00 noon. The Caucus Room was filled with clicking cameras and flashing light bulbs as John F. Kennedy stood there shuffling his papers. Then he pushed back his hair nervously, managed a slight smile and began to speak:

"I am announcing today my candidacy for the Presidency of the United States," he said.

"The Presidency is the most powerful office in the Free World. Through the leadership can come a more vital life for our people. In it are centered the hopes of the globe around us for freedom and a more secure life. For it is in the Executive Branch that the most crucial decisions of this century must be made in the next four years—how to end or alter the burdensome arms race, where Soviet gains already threaten our very existence—how to maintain freedom and order in the newly emerging nations—how to rebuild the stature of American science and education—how to prevent the collapse of our farm economy and the decay of our cities—how to achieve without further inflation or unemployment, expanded economic growth benefiting all Americans—how to give direction to our traditional moral purpose, awakening every American to the dangers and opportunities that confront us."

It was on these issues, he said, that the American people must make their fateful choice for their future.

He felt a close relation to the American people because "in the past forty-nine months, I have toured every state in the Union, and I have talked to Democrats in all walks of life." Aware that there had been no other Catholic Presidential candidate from the Senate in the 1900's, he felt required to say, "My candidacy is therefore based upon the conviction that I can win both the nomination and election."

Introducing a new theme, he threw out to all of the other contenders the following challenge: "I believe that any Democratic aspirant to this important nomination should be willing to submit to the voters his views, record and competence in a series of primary contests. I am, therefore, announcing my intentions of filing . . . in various primaries."

He went on, "For eighteen years, I have been in the

service of the United States, first as a Naval officer in the Pacific during World War Two and for the past fourteen years a member of Congress. In the last twenty years, I have traveled in nearly every continent and country—from Leningrad to Saigon, from Bucharest to Lima. From all of this, I have developed an image of America as fulfilling a noble and historic role as the defender of freedom in a time of maximum peril—and of the American people as confident, courageous and persevering.

"It is with this image that I begin this campaign."

I am sure that the farthest thought from Lyndon B. Johnson's mind at that time was that John F. Kennedy would be the man to beat in the convention. But, whether either of them admitted it or not, the duel between these two men had already started. The clash was especially harsh because each man knew that this was a make or break year as far as his political future was concerned. Mr. Kennedy knew that if he fell short of his goal, a prospect he would never accept, politicians would say that his religion was the cause—not his youth. He was sure that this would mean another long wait before another Catholic would try to break through the religious barrier. It was an anti-Catholic barrier, first set up when the Puritans landed, and greatly strengthened by Al Smith's defeat. Yet, Lyndon Johnson also faced the divisive problems that remain in America since the first cannon ball was fired at Fort Sumter. The Majority

Leader was seen as a Southerner, as nothing more than a regional politician. He had taken courageous and carefully calculated steps to remove that barrier by refusing to sign the southern manifesto against the Supreme Court's school desegregation ruling, and he supported the moderate Kennedy-Ives bill to regulate union abuses, despite the fact that his friends back home were snorting about the need for a much harsher crackdown on unions. If Johnson were to be unsuccessful at the convention, right at the peak of his power as a legislative master, and even after he had modified his voting patterns, then it would seem to be clear that he was being rejected only because he was a Southerner. If he could not jump this hurdle now, it was unlikely he could do so in the future and still hold his group together in Texas. Turbulent Texas, the uncertainties of his home base, his bitter memory of winning his Senate seat by a mere 87 votes—all these were reasons for this thinking that 1960 was the year to move.

And continually in Senator Johnson's thoughts, I am sure, was the fact that the next President might be more aggressive than Eisenhower. This would do away with a good deal of Johnson's ability to use his Senate post to command attention and to exert leadership.

"And you must not forget," someone added at the time, "his old friend and sponsor, Speaker Sam Rayburn, is getting up in years and may not be around to give him aid and assistance through another Administration. The one thing that Mr. Sam wants more than anything else is to see a Texan sitting in the President's chair."

The two men, Johnson and Kennedy, were fighting a personal battle of political survival, and at the same time were involved in a giant contest to overcome different forms of prejudice. Senator Kennedy had to kill the myth that a Catholic President would be an errand boy for the Pope and would trade the gold in Fort Knox for a supply of holy water; Senator Johnson had to show, somehow, that a Southerner could rise above his region and take liberal positions on vital issues. Their battleground would be the Democratic Convention of 1960. That was about the only fact on which they agreed.

The timing and content of their announcements showed their different styles and strategies very clearly. Senator Johnson timed his formal announcement for July 5th, six months after Senator Kennedy had made his announcement and just one week before the gavel would sound the opening of the Democratic Convention. In fact, when Senator Johnson announced, delegates were already arriving at Los Angeles, and the hotel rooms were beginning to add clouds of cigar smoke to the Los Angeles smog.

By the time Mr. Johnson called the unsurprised correspondents to his announcement conference in the impressive theater in the New Senate Office Building,

Mr. Kennedy was the front-runner and chief contender in the race for the Presidency. The political implication of Mr. Johnson's timing was clear. He preferred to play national Presidential politics as if it were cloak room politics in the Senate, at which he was the acknowledged master. By his late announcement, he could say that it had been necessary for him to be on the job in the Senate, and, therefore, he had been unable to get around the country and expose himself in primaries as Mr. Kennedy had. This was part of his strategy. He also believed that if he could keep the decisions in the back rooms, where his footwork was best, he could win.

"The forces of evil," Johnson sternly warned, in a slap at Senator Kennedy's age, "will have no mercy for innocence, no gallantry for inexperience." He also declared that no Democratic Convention could permit itself to be bound in advance to any one man. Woodrow Wilson, Al Smith, and Franklin D. Roosevelt had all been nominated after the first ballot, he reminded his listeners.

"I am not going to go plowing through 179 million Americans, pushing aside other Senators and Governors and Congressmen to shout 'Look at me and nobody else,' " the Majority Leader drawled.

"Those who have engaged in active campaigns since January have missed hundreds of votes. This I could not do—for my country or party. Someone had to tend the store."

These men were bound to clash and they did. This is the nature of political combat, and there is no use denying it happened or overlooking the consequences by pretending that either Kennedy or Johnson took great care not to embitter their future relations, or that they were even considering modifying any position or tactic so that they could take the Vice Presidency on the other man's ticket. Most of us who lived it, saw clearly that this was a fight to the finish, fought with gloves off.

Kennedy was off and running in the primaries and Mr. Johnson was trying to score by his "minding the store" theme. Every time Senator Kennedy would leave Washington, Senator Johnson would charge that he was an "absentee Senator." The primaries were "put in for a purpose," Mr. Kennedy shot back, "to give the people a voice—a far more satisfactory system than picking somebody in a hotel room in Los Angeles." Then Mr. Kennedy added, "Mr. Johnson would never enter the primaries. He doesn't play politics this way."

There was no question that the Texan worked hard and was determined to get things done. He became extremely disturbed when Senators were unavailable for quorum or roll calls. To have them constantly at his finger-tips was part of the bargaining. At one time, during a fight to break the filibuster in February 1960, he actually had cots placed in the cloakrooms so that he would know where the Senators were in case he needed them immediately. He said that he was making this fight to please civil-rights minded Democrats.

Mr. Kennedy was also practical. He knew that the established party leaders would never permit him to get the nomination. His only recourse was to go to the people, and to prove that his youth and his religion would not stand in his way. He didn't want party leaders, like Rayburn and Truman, who were sure a Catholic could not win, to veto him by just saying what they thought.

He also felt that a new era in American political leadership was on the horizon. The primaries were one way of persuading the people to throw off the dead hand of the past. In an article in Life magazine in 1957, he had written: "With a new breed of respected, dynamic professional politicians coming into prominence, we can no longer afford to continue in official party positions tired or tarnished holdovers from another era—men who keep busily attending meetings, filing gloomy forecasts, and complaints, and fighting zealously to hold on to their positions."

Kennedy understood Johnson's need to "mind the store" and knew he couldn't enter all the primaries, but still he felt that what applied to him also applied to Mr. Johnson.

"Johnson," Kennedy said some time later, "had to prove that a Southerner could win in the North, just as I had to prove a Catholic could win in heavily

Protestant states. Could you imagine me, having entered no primaries trying to tell the leaders that being a Catholic was no handicap? When Lyndon said he could win in the North, but could offer no concrete evidence, his claims couldn't be taken seriously."

Kennedy answered Senator Johnson's contempt for the primaries by saying, "Primaries are the ordinary voter's chance to speak his own mind, to cast his own vote—regardless of what he may be told to do by some other self-appointed spokesman for his party, city, church, union or other organization." With this faith, he marched into the primary battlefields of Wisconsin where not an important state political leader supported him. As he went along, he also reminded the other candidates that "for fifty years no Republican or Democrat has reached the White House without entering and winning at least one contested primary."

Mr. Johnson was constantly drumming the charge of Mr. Kennedy being an "absentee Senator" in his statements to the press. We even heard that his aides and campaign workers were so worked up over this charge, which they thought was tremendously appealing, that they mailed to Democratic delegates Republican material damaging to Mr. Kennedy. What they mailed was an open letter from scrappy Pennsylvania Republican Senator Hugh Scott, accusing candidate Kennedy of being the "absentee Senator." "You know," one of Kennedy's aides said, "this is really carrying bipartisanship pretty far." There had been complaints from Senators that the leadership seemed to prefer to have a Republican in the White House. In that way they could take credit for the victories and blame the opposition for failures.

Mr. Johnson and Mr. Sam were not only "minding the store," they also were buttonholing their friends and allies in Congress, who in turn began the spade work back home. A national magazine pinned the ugly badge "wheeler-dealer" on the Senate Democratic Leader.

Transferring all this wheeling and dealing of the cloak room to the back rooms of the convention put Mr. Johnson into a very suspicious atmosphere. When things are done behind closed doors, regardless of how honorable they are, there is always that element of suspicion. Therefore, when controversial Adam Clayton Powell, Harlem's Congressman, came out for Johnson for the Presidency, eyebrows were raised. Not everyone seemed to believe he did so on a popular demand from his Harlem constituents.

Mr. Kennedy charged bluntly, "My chief competitors in the convention remain safely on the sidelines, hoping to gain the nomination through manipulation."

Mr. Johnson, for his part, had more solid reasons for staying out of the primaries than his expressed idealistic reason of serving the country by "minding the store." He was always fearful that there would be a small turnout for his speeches and often complained privately that the big cities didn't really welcome him. In polls and in instances where, by chance, his name was matched against Kennedy on ballots the results were alarming.

In Indiana, where Hoosier Senator Vance Hartke urged Johnson to enter the primary, public poll taker Lou Harris found that less than 40 percent of the voters of that state knew enough about the Texas Senator to express an opinion. A majority of those who had heard of him were uncertain of how they felt about him. Most of them called him a "politician's politician." Harris, in defining this term, had this to say: "As a politician's politician, a man is known and even admired for his cool, calculating skill but never for his warmth toward the rank and file of people. He is a cunning and clever individual, but not one who evoked the kind of warmth or confidence of which Presidential majorities are born."

Mr. Kennedy did generate enthusiasm by entering the primaries. This was apparent from the write-in votes for President in the State of Illinois on April 12, 1960. Some 34,000 people wrote in the name John F. Kennedy, while only 442 singled out Lyndon B. Johnson. And to the amazement of all—Adlai Stevenson, a former Governor of Illinois—only received 8,000 votes.

On a Gallup poll a little later, the three men were pitted against Nixon. Kennedy was 54% to Nixon's

46%; Stevenson 48%—Nixon 52%; and Johnson 46%—Nixon 54%. On one of his trips away from the Senate, when he spoke in Pittsburgh, the Mayor of that city told Mr. Johnson that he thought he would make a good nominee. But facts were facts. In a preferential primary in that industrial city, Kennedy received almost 76,000 write-ins to Johnson's 745.

There was nothing Mr. Johnson could do about the primary in Oregon. The only way a candidate could keep from having his name on the ballot was to file a disclaimer, similar to the one Adlai Stevenson filed, which read, "I am not now and do not intend to become a candidate for President." Mr. Johnson could not go that far, but one of his aides did say that he would not campaign in that state. His name was on the ballot and Mr. Kennedy not only swamped Mr. Johnson in that primary, but he swept past Oregon's own Presidential candidate, Senator Wayne Morse.

Mr. Sam, however, tried to discount the Kennedy victories in the six primaries and reassured Mr. Johnson that he had support all over the country, with his strongest support in the South and the border states. He hoped that Senator Johnson would carry between 450 and 500 votes to the convention and then on the fourth or fifth ballot he would win. That's what his pocket full of political IOU's added up to.

CHAPTER III

Rustling Delegates

NATURALLY, everyone in our office was happy and excited at the outcome of the primaries. I said to Mr. Kennedy, "They can't stop you now." "Oh, yes, they can," he replied. "We still have plenty of work to do." He explained, "Winning in the primaries gave us a big psychological boost, of course. But only a small percentage of convention delegates are chosen and firmly committed this way. It is up to our liaison men to get to the delegates."

I soon learned that Mr. Kennedy had begun moving into an area where, according to the press, Mr. Johnson was the master politician, the greatest ever to come down the pike. The youthful Mr. Kennedy might be able to attract young people because of his fresh boyish look and glamorous appeal, but when it came to hard-nose politics, talking to delegates and horse-trading, well, he just wasn't in Mr. Johnson's league. Mr. Johnson also had working for him all those old pros in the Senate and the House for whom he had done favors or made deals. They were the people who knew how to talk to the delegates.

Later, after that struggle for delegates faded into the past, a version of history persisted in picturing Mr. Johnson and his men as master of the political pros, with Kennedy and his men neophytes in that department. The facts of what happened in those party caucuses are entirely contrary to such a version of events.

Mr. Kennedy had to rely on friends, contacts, liaison men, and others to get votes in the various delegations. Since the early part of 1959 he and his staff had been laying the groundwork and discussing the strategy to be used in this part of the campaign to gain delegate votes. In early 1960 things seemed to be going along in the same haphazard manner that all of our operations had. I could never really understand how our affairs turned out as well as they did. There was always so much confusion, so many telephones ringing, so many people coming in—going out—and always, always, the mail was staggering.

No one seemed to know what anyone else was doing, and we seemed to have more than our share of confusion. Underneath, of course, there was organization and directed movement. I noticed, for example, that all of the men chosen to contact the delegates were old friends and associates of either Mr. Kennedy or a member of his family. I had never seen so many roommates, from so many schools, show up to help out. They were not old pros or "pols," but sincere young men who were inspired by the challenge Mr. Kennedy was making. They were highly motivated, so to them time meant nothing.

And time did mean nothing to all of us who worked for Mr. Kennedy. The clock seemed to spin around, yet, though we worked very hard, for very long hours, no one minded. There was a wonderful air around us which was much more important.

The method of operating would have made Mr. Johnson laugh. Each liaison man was assigned to a part of the country, even though it may have been strange to him. For instance, friendly, affable Lem Billings, an old friend and a roommate from Mr. Kennedy's days at Choate, a native of Maryland, was sent to Wisconsin. Since I knew he was no more familiar with Wisconsin politics than with the customs of head hunters in New Guinea, I asked the reasoning behind this strange assignment. The liaison men explained to me, "If a man is a stranger to the people, he is not biased. He is not connected or identified with any faction. He does not have ties with any organization. He is a free agent able to put together a brand new organization . . . not one that is tied in with all of the old pros. And also they are filled with a fresh spirit and enthusiasm and this is catching." As it turned out some of the liaison men made such good friends that they were given testimonial dinners after Kennedy's election, in areas where once they were strangers.

Each week reports from all parts of the country arrived from these liaison men. As they came across my desk, I read them and made sure that Mr. Kennedy would see them. Some reports were short and to the point, while others were full of detail and local color. In one town, the liaison men called at a delegate's office and, as he came out, noticed a cowboy sitting in the waiting room, all dressed up in full regalia, complete with dressy cowboy boots and a ten-gallon hat. Our scout was somewhat surprised, since it was an area where cowboys are even less common than Indians. This particular cowhand was also wearing a "yellow rose" insignia, further evidence that he was one of Mr. Johnson's "Texas Rangers," as we called them. Our men were called the "whiz kids," and their only noticeable difference from the ordinary man on the street was the PT-boat tie clasp they all wore, inscribed with the words "Kennedy 60."

It was difficult to keep up with the organization of the other candidates because I was so busy in our own campaign. But I did know that sometime in October 1959, old pals, Speaker Sam Rayburn and Governor Price Daniel, had formed an "unofficial" Johnson for President Committee in Dallas. Price Daniel was so conservative that he bolted the party in 1952 rather than support Adlai Stevenson. In his campaign for

Governor, he struck out more at Walter Reuther and the NAACP than at his Republican opponent.

It was out of this base of operation, later moved to Austin, that the small group of delegate scouts, the "Texas Rangers," operated. One of the most effective men on Mr. Johnson's team was handsome John B. Connally, who was so inspired by Mr. Johnson that he tried to speak like him and to mimic his political manner. Mr. Connally was just as conservative as Governor Daniel, as was his assistant, Marvin Watson, of the Lone Star Steel Company.

"John Connally and Cliff Carter from Johnson's office in Austin have been moved to Washington," Steve Smith told me one morning. "So," he went on, "we will be sending you any press releases and statements that they issue. Be sure that Kennedy sees them." It wasn't long before press releases started to appear. One of the first implied that Johnson is the greatest Majority Leader in the history of the United States, while Kennedy is nothing but a boy.

I must say that Senator Johnson had excellent press coverage. Whenever he made a move in the Senate the headlines proclaimed "Johnson did this" or "Johnson did that." He really stood out as "Mr. Senator" or "Mr. Democratic Leader," and he gained the reputation of a man who got his own way, for whom manipulating men was like a game. He seemed to like nothing better than getting a man in a corner and giving him the famous "Johnson treatment." He would frown, he would smile, he would appeal, and he would use sweet talk. And all of the time he would pound home the theme that they should do it "for good old Lyndon, and for the good of the country." If persuasive adjectives failed, he would use his hands. He would hug the victim, pat him, grip his arm with a clutch that was as unbreakable, and just about as comfortable, as a bulldog's bite. Some people called him a "sleight-of-hand artist."

We, too, waged the battle of press releases. Ours, too, were biased, but Mr. Kennedy was more interested in getting ideas across to the people, about what he would do and what he stood for, than he was in attacking Mr. Johnson.

Walter Jenkins, an agreeable, friendly man, worked out of Johnson's Senate office. Walter, who had been Mr. Johnson's Administrative Assistant since his days in the House, was a very close personal friend of Mr. Johnson and his family. His chief duty in the campaign, I was told, was to act as a bridge to Mr. Sam and friendly Congressmen. His job was to prod them, to keep them on the ball in working on delegates. This was fine if it worked, but politicians have a tendency to inflate reports and, since they knew Mr. Johnson wanted only things that looked favorable, that's what they did. So Mr. Johnson was getting reports on his delegate strength that bore as much relation to realism as the fellow who planted toads and expected to grow toadstools.

One thing that always fascinated me was the number of offices that Mr. Johnson maintained. He had two in Texas, one in the Ambassador Hotel in Washington, two, and then three, in the Senate Office Building, the usual office in the basement of the Capitol and, of course, his plush Majority Leader's Office right outside of the Senate floor. In this office, his able assistant was the Secretary to the Democratic Majority, Bobby Baker. Bobby, like Connally and Walter Jenkins, liked to model himself after Mr. Johnson and to do things he knew would please him. Bobby even named two of his children after him—Lyndon John and Lynda.

Bobby was certainly one of the busiest men in the Johnson push for the Presidency since his was the job of keeping the Senators in line for his boss. I would often run into him at the snack bar hurriedly bolting a sandwich on days he wasn't over at the Quorum Club. He looked very young and always appeared neat and trim, with hair so slick it looked as though it had been painted on his head.

It was through Bobby's office that changes were made on the various Senate committees. This was one of the levers that could prove to be useful in getting a Senator to use his influence on convention delegates. Also Baker counted noses for Mr. Johnson when a bill was under consideration. The report he turned in sometimes meant life or death for a bill, and the report might also determine whether or not Mr. Johnson would make a real fight for it.

Despite whatever else may be said about Mr. Baker, he was very efficient at this aspect of his job. No bill, during Bobby Baker's time, was ever lost because of an incorrect head-count or because Senators could not be found in time.

There was another area in which Bobby was very influential and that was in the Senate Campaign Committee. As secretary to this committee, he had a hand in doling out funds to Senators for their campaigns. Although these funds were for all the Democratic Senators who were running for office that year, most of it was somehow showing up in the states where Mr. Johnson had his greatest hopes for gaining convention delegates. Mr. Kennedy protested, but that is as far as he got.

There was some talk about the pressure of persuasion that the Kennedy men were using. This was a hard fought game and Mr. Kennedy never went into anything without playing it hard. "You have to win to put your ideas into action," he would say. "Just as the road to hell is paved with good intentions," he remarked, "the pages of history are studded with countries that disappeared because they couldn't turn their good ideas into action." As one newspaper man said, "He has the toughness and the touch of ruthlessness necessary in politics."

Mr. Johnson threw the charge at Mr. Kennedy that he was soft on communism and could not stand up to Khrushchev. Mr. Kennedy reminded Johnson of his successful past campaigns, like the one against Henry

Cabot Lodge, and of the 1956 Convention, when he lost by only an eyelash. If that showed weakness, he wanted to know what you had to do to show strength.

The maneuvering and rustling for delegates was getting more and more exciting. Through the battle of press releases Senator Johnson was insisting that Kennedy was strictly an Easterner, with no chance at all in the South nor any appeal in the West. Mr. Kennedy tried to hem in Johnson in the South, picturing him as merely a regional candidate.

Mr. Kennedy felt that it would be necessary for him to win on the first ballot. In order to do that he would have to get 761 votes. At the beginning, the best count we could get was around 600 to Johnson's 350 to 400 votes. If Johnson could pick up another 150 votes, he would be able to stop Kennedy on the first ballot. If that were possible, he could start bargaining toward the kind of West and South combinations that had brought nominations in other conventions. The bargaining would then start with the old pros in the cities and Mr. Johnson would have the edge. Everyone agreed that it was "first ballot or bust."

The primaries were over and whenever he wasn't needed in the Senate, Mr. Kennedy took to the air in his private plane, the *Caroline*, to go out and do a little rustling of delegates himself. Mr. Johnson also was flying around trying to win friends and influence delegates. He flew to New York to see that old pol, Carmine DeSapio, though he knew before he went that DeSapio was friendly. He also called on Governor Robert Meyner of New Jersey who also implied his support. He didn't do so well with Governor Lawrence of Pennsylvania since the Governor wanted to see what his dear old friend Adlai Stevenson was going to do.

At the beginning of June, with still another month to go, the polls were showing Kennedy with 620 votes on the first ballot, Johnson 510, Symington 140, Humphrey 100, and Adlai Stevenson 75. Mr. Johnson was on the outside rail and seemed to be moving up.

He made a trip to Iowa and when he came out from visiting with Governor Herschel C. Loveless, he said Iowa was in the bag for him. Mr. Kennedy went to Iowa, too. In Des Moines, he won over Iowa's Democratic State Chairman, Duke Norbert. And at Los Angeles, Governor Loveless and Duke Norbert led most of their state's 26 votes into the Kennedy column before the balloting was over.

In another state, Montana, Mr. Johnson announced that Senator Mansfield was for him. Mr. Kennedy had the very popular and active candidate for the United States Senate, Lee Metcalf, working for him. Mr. Kennedy spoke to the Democratic Convention near Last Chance Gulch and when the votes were counted out in Los Angeles, Kennedy received 10 out of the 17 Montana delegates' votes.

The race was exciting in many states. Congressman Stewart L. Udall from Arizona quietly organized his state for Mr. Kennedy, unbeknownst to two very good friends of Mr. Johnson, Senator Carl Hayden and former Majority Leader Ernest McFarland. When Speaker Rayburn found out what Udall had done, he was soundly reprimanded. The same happened in Wyoming and Colorado where two young devoted men—Teno Roncalio and Joe Dolan—undercut the leadership.

Of course we didn't win them all. There were times when Mr. Johnson and his Rangers did better than Mr. Kennedy and our people. When Mr. Kennedy's men raided Mr. Johnson's neighboring state of New Mexico, Mr. Johnson's friends in the Senate, Chavez and Anderson, helped hold the delegations for him. Mr. Kennedy, however, made a flying visit to the New Mexico convention and pulled four votes right out from under Mr. Johnson's nose.

In Oklahoma, in spite of the fact that Senator Kennedy had Governor Edmondson working for him, Mr. Johnson's old buddy in the United States Senate, Senator Robert Kerr, held all of Oklahoma's votes for him.

The same was true in Kentucky. Johnson's able friend, former Senator Earle Clements, then Kentucky's Highway Commissioner, helped freeze Mr. Kennedy out of that delegation.

The rustling, the pressuring, the wheeling and dealing continued. The Johnson men were using "Johnson tactics." They passed the word at the Governor's Conference on June 28th that if the Governors declared for

Mr. Kennedy there would be no campaign funds for them. But such tactics are often two-edged, as the Johnson forces discovered when Governor G. Mennen Williams of Michigan told the press about the threats he had received and then publicly endorsed Mr. Kennedy.

What had happened to the old pols? Mr. Kennedy's spectacular success in their kind of politics had really shocked them. They had been frozen out of the primaries and now they had met their match in the back rooms too. It had always been said that Mr. Kennedy was a charmer on the platform, a spinner of phrases, and a wit. But as far as dealing with the rough and tumble, hard-hitting pros in politics, he wasn't supposed to hold a candle to Mr. Johnson. Yet, now, it was his figure that was emerging from the cigar smoke. It was almost unfair.

A very interesting article by Hugh Sidey appeared in *Life* magazine much later which commented, "There is a persistent legend that Lyndon B. Johnson is the world's best politician. He is regarded by many of his enemies as well as his friends as having almost mystical ability to understand the polls and the pols, to know how to wage and win elections, to pursue and persuade the indifferent and the doubtful. But in fact, this evaluation is imprecise and highly misleading . . . it is still a matter of wonderment to students of L.B.J. that a man so adept in other forms can remain so clumsy in national campaigning. Back in 1960 when all those

Democrats had been seeking the Presidential nomination, Johnson was the most inept of all the losers. While Kennedy went out into the country and gathered the delegates, L.B.J. relied on his Senate cronies—many of whom had long since lost touch with their states—to deliver the goods to him. He accepted political advice from the likes of Bobby Baker, who may have known how to manage in the Senate cloakroom, but had no understanding of how to work in the open spaces. Johnson always has had a singular reluctance to believe bad news. In 1960, he preferred to rely on the dubious promises and evaluations of a host of second-raters who had attached themselves to him in search for power. He was, of course, clobbered."

There is one moral to be drawn from an accurate picture of the Kennedy–Johnson duel for delegates which is very important, because it affects Kennedy's rendezvous with the youth of America and his lasting influence on them.

Every politician, whether successful or not, whether he intends it or not, is by both words and behavior, a teacher to youth. Some capture the imagination of youth and inspire them to devote a year to a Peace Corps project in Nigeria, accept a career in government service, or become fine political leaders. Others fail to capture the imagination of youth, but nevertheless young people draw conclusions from their actions and words.

Mr. Kennedy had a clear message for young people.

He wanted them to feel that politics was a noble profession. His message to youth was that whatever anybody says, and however many examples there are to the contrary, hard-headed politics can be combined with high-level achievement in public life. Both are dependent on each other. He warned against listening to the cynics who say politics is always crooked and bad and that a typical politician shakes your hand before election and pulls your leg afterward. Actually the low road in politics doesn't guarantee victory, but, rather, ultimate defeat.

In this pre-convention campaign, Senator Kennedy seemed to symbolize an open, though hard-hitting determination to win political office. Senator Johnson, on the other hand, came across to the youth of America as an old-fashioned, behind-the-scenes politician, with whom they could not align themselves.

When Mr. Sam was just leaving his ranch to go to Los Angeles for the Convention, he was asked bluntly: "Mr. Sam, do you really believe Lyndon will win the nomination?" He said, "Well, if we can get through the first roll call, he has a chance. Jack could win it on the first ballot. He has worked hard and has made many trips. Everywhere he goes he leaves behind an organization. There are some good young fellows working for him too. Lyndon just hasn't had the time to do this."

Although Mr. Rayburn expressed some apprehension over the outcome, Mr. Johnson must not have shared his opinion, because he announced his candidacy on July 5th, just six days before the opening of the convention. There were still some "Stop Kennedy" maneuvers in the works, upon which he must have been relying heavily. And, after all, there was some rustling left to do. State caucuses were bracing themselves and putting up the storm shutters—they were about to get the "Johnson treatment."

CHAPTER IV

Stop Kennedy

ALL DURING this exciting race for the nomination the papers were full of cartoons about Mr. Kennedy and Mr. Johnson. It heightened the rivalry between them and it also portrayed the kind of campaigns they were waging. There was definitely a movement on Mr. Johnson's part to stop Kennedy. The cartoon that really explained the "Stop Kennedy" movement was called "Stop Kennedy Club." In the picture were club members Hubert, Sam, Morse, Lyndon, H.S.T., Stu, Den Mother (Mrs. Roosevelt), K.K.K., Dixiecrats, and Hoffa.

"It is not unusual for candidates running behind to join together in order to stop the front runner," Mr. Kennedy said. "But I am disturbed over the 'gang up' tactics that are being used. And I am disappointed in Mr. Johnson for his behind-the-scenes maneuvering of this movement."

Politics make strange bedfellows and it was apparent that Mr. Johnson was not about to let a forty-two-year-old junior Senator snatch the Presidency away from him. But what I couldn't understand was how Adlai Stevenson, Hubert Humphrey and Stuart Symington got pulled into this movement. None of them seemed to be that kind of politician. However, you never know what makes a politician tick. They all have terrific egos. And then sometimes, they become obligated. There was an interesting example in Wisconsin. It wasn't until it was apparent that Humphrey might get defeated that Mr. Johnson sent James Rowe, Jr., one of his close political advisors, to help Humphrey. And there was no doubt that Mr. Johnson encouraged Mr. Humphrey to run in the West Virginia primary. Almost certainly his purpose was not to "be kind to Hubert Humphrey," but to use the ambitious Minnesotan to stop the Kennedy drive. Both Johnson and Humphrey felt that a Catholic candidate did not have a chance in West Virginia.

James Rowe again showed up in West Virginia and when someone asked Mr. Humphrey what implications should be drawn from Rowe's backing, he replied with a grin, "Well, I don't know what kind of implications you want to draw, but you know he is a close friend of Lyndon's and Lyndon has said all along he would not be a candidate."

Everyone was wondering where Mr. Humphrey was getting his money to campaign, because he was a man of very modest means. Then we learned that Mr. Johnson was asking some of his New York friends, men who couldn't stand Mr. Kennedy, to send Humphrey some money quietly. Eventually, it was even reported in the newspapers that such money was coming to Humphrey from wealthy New Yorkers, though this was not considerd in later accounts of how the "Kennedy machine" defeated Mr. Humphrey in West Virginia.

Another thing that Mr. Johnson did for Mr. Humphrey was to get his friend, Earle Clements, former U.S. Senator from Kentucky, to go over to West Virginia to speak for him. It was about this time that Mr. Kennedy came up with one of his aces. He brought Franklin D. Roosevelt, Jr., of New York to stump the state for him and speak to the Mountaineers. What a tremendous boost he gave to the campaign. These people loved Mr. Roosevelt's father, the late FDR, and that name was pure magic to them.

In spite of all the behind-the-scenes maneuvering by Mr. Johnson and his followers the news that kept coming out of West Virginia gave Mr. Kennedy a slight edge. Only three days remained before they would go to the polls, but no one dared to believe that a Catholic could win there. Then came the startling news that Mr. Johnson was going to enter the state himself. He was going to speak in Clarksburg. We immediately wondered how he was going to handle this situation. All along he had been helping Hubert Humphrey, but his colleague in the Senate, Robert Byrd of West Virginia, was urging all of the delegates in his state to line up for Mr. Johnson. Therefore, we reasoned that if Johnson didn't talk for himself, he would have to talk out of both sides of his mouth.

He did go to Clarksburg and he made an impassioned speech about how important it was to stay at the helm of the ship of state and not go around entering primaries. Then came the shocker. He not only reprimanded Mr. Kennedy for neglecting his Senatorial duties, he also reprimanded Mr. Humphrey. He repeated time and time again that he had remained in Washington for the good of the country to "mind the store."

The outcome of the primary is history now. What started out to be a drive to "Stop Kennedy" in West Virginia ended up by "stopping Humphrey" because, after it was all over, Mr. Humphrey withdrew from the race. He said he was going to concentrate on his race for the United States Senate though he remained true to Mr. Johnson, his sometime supporter. Humphrey held out to the very last moment at the convention by refusing to release his delegates—delegates that might have gone to Mr. Kennedy.

There is something strange about human nature. When people feel that there is a "gang up" movement going on, they root for the underdog, almost by instinct. It is not a feeling that can be created by the individual himself. Instead it comes about through a series of events. This feeling for Mr. Kennedy must have seeped down into some of Mr. Johnson's offices because many of his employes were rushing over to our workshop offices, volunteering to work for us after hours. They were willing to do any kind of menial tasks like folding letters, stuffing envelopes, or licking stamps.

We learned many things about Mr. Johnson from these "volunteers." For one thing he was extremely temperamental and, since the West Virginia primary, very irritable. Whenever he came into his office and had a "mad on," the feeling went through the entire office like an electric shock and everyone "froze" at their desks. This was even true in the workshop offices, even though he never stopped by to see them. The one thing he did was to use the telephone, and it was not unusual for them to pick up the receiver and hear his thunderous voice blasting away for something he thought they should have done.

"Do you know," they said, "one minute he would give one of his aides a tremendous tongue-lashing and then he would turn right around and give him an expensive gift and say to him 'you know you are my right arm.' " He ran the length of the keyboard in a matter of minutes. They also said that sometimes he would come into his office and be just as docile as a lamb and would call all the girls "honey." But they never knew how long this mood was going to last. Senator Johnson flashed his moods off and on like an electric light-switch, and an aide never knew whether he was going to brag about him to a visitor or say that he didn't know enough to get out of the rain.

"Boy, is he impulsive," they said. "He never lets

anyone know what he is going to do. And if someone suggests that he is going to do a certain thing and he finds it out, he will just do the opposite." We also learned that he handled legislation the same way. He would never say in advance what stand he was going to take on a bill. And once again, if news leaked out about a certain bill, he might block it completely.

As far as speaking engagements were concerned, if he accepted an invitation, the program chairman was never sure that he would be there, because at the very last minute he might decide to do something else.

The volunteers also said that it was not unusual for Mr. Johnson to be sitting in his private plane heading for Washington, to call out to his pilot and tell him that he had changed his mind, that he was not going to Washington after all. He would tell the pilot to turn the plane around and fly back to the LBJ Ranch in Texas.

While Mr. Johnson was changing his mind, Mr. Kennedy was working on someone else to change his mind. That man was Adlai Stevenson. "What is Adlai Stevenson going to do?" Mr. Kennedy would say. "I think it is more important to the success of the party to be nominated by the liberals than by the South." And then he would add, "I had hoped that Adlai would give me some positive assurance of support before the convention, especially now that Hubert Humphrey has withdrawn from the race."

Time and again Mr. Kennedy tried to arrange

luncheon or dinner meetings with Mr. Stevenson up in Cambridge, Massachusetts, but they never materialized. He even passed the word along to him that surely he realized from the polls that he himself didn't have a chance of being nominated. But that seemed to be one of Mr. Stevenson's traits—he couldn't make up his mind.

Finally, it was arranged for Mr. Kennedy to call on the Governor at his home in Libertyville, Illinois. However, before this meeting, Adlai Stevenson came to Washington to testify before one of the committees, and while he was in town he had a long talk with Mr. Johnson. It didn't take Kennedy long to find out when he stopped at Libertyville soon thereafter that Adlai did not want to give his support to anyone. He said that he would be betraying his trust to other candidates if he were to give his support to Mr. Kennedy, since he had told everyone that he would remain neutral. Mr. Kennedy was very upset by Stevenson's attitude, but there was nothing that he could do about it.

Adlai Stevenson must have received the "Johnson treatment" because James Rowe, who was now back in Washington working for Mr. Johnson, was also working closely with the Stevenson Washington forces—Senator Mike Monroney and his hard-driving assistant, Tom Finney. Whether Mr. Stevenson liked it or not, he had become enmeshed into the "Stop Kennedy" web. "He is really helping Mr. Johnson by doing this," Senator Kennedy said.

The third man to be caught up in the "Stop Kennedy" movement was former President Harry S. Truman. President Truman had said he was for Senator Stuart Symington, but he was also very opposed to the idea of having John Kennedy, a Catholic, as the Democratic nominee. When they asked Speaker Rayburn if he had discussed the convention with Mr. Truman he replied, "Yes, Harry wrote me, and he said we ought to get together on this thing. He likes Johnson, but he also thinks Symington would make a good President." Speaker Rayburn and Mr. Johnson agreed wholeheartedly with Truman about "stopping Kennedy" and they no doubt had that "get-together," because just two days before the 4th of July the firecrackers started. The networks were announcing that President Truman had called a televised press conference in Independence, Missouri to announce to the people why he was not going to the Democratic Convention. What a time for the TV in our office to be out of order!

After a great deal of frantic calling, Herbert Klein, Administrative Assistant to Vice President Richard M. Nixon came across the hall and graciously invited us to come over to their office to listen to the salty ex-President. It was like music to the ears of the Republicans: a former President was going to blast a member of his own party on a national TV hook-up. It really was unbelievable, but then so were many of the other maneuvers. Finally, Mr. Truman faced the TV cameras and announced that he was not going to attend the convention, because—and then he implied—Mr. Kennedy had rigged it. His language was caustic. Somewhere along the line he accused Kennedy of not being dry behind the ears. "Senator," Truman bitingly asked, "are you certain that you are quite ready for the country . . . May I urge you to be patient," he asserted . . . "Are you certain . . . the country is ready for you?"

Mr. Kennedy certainly knew what the country was thinking because he had been traveling from one coast to the other for the past three years, while Mr. Truman was in semi-retirement. Still, the former President proposed several new names to be considered at the convention, though his main purpose was to attack Mr. Kennedy. The more he spoke the more infuriated we became and, as soon as the press conference ended, Mr. Kennedy was on the telephone from Hyannis Port, Massachusetts, where he had gone to spend the 4th of July with his family. He was steaming. The telephone wires were red hot all that day and most of the next, demanding equal TV time and preparing an answer.

The harder the blows, the stronger Mr. Kennedy became. That was one of his great strengths. And the answers that he gave to these attacks were always on a high level. We had no fear, as we sat before the TV on the 4th of July. We knew that Mr. Kennedy would not falter.

In answer to the question "was the country ready

for him?" he said: . . . It is "time for a new generation of leadership to cope with new problems and new opportunities." He would not, he said, "step aside at anyone's request." And then came the mightiest thrust of all. "If fourteen years of major elective office is insufficient experience, that rules out all but three of the names put forward by Truman and all but a handful of American Presidents, and every President of the twentieth century—including Wilson, Roosevelt, and Truman." The one thing the opposition had forgotten was how well Mr. Kennedy came through on TV!

At the time Mr. Kennedy was busy preparing his answer to Mr. Truman, John B. Connally, who was now working in the Johnson headquarters in Los Angeles, had cooked up another slashing attack. "My boy John," as Mr. Johnson called him, teamed up with Mrs. India Edwards, formerly head of the women's division of the Democratic National Committee, and together they called a press conference. On the 4th of July!

"Mr. Kennedy is a very sick man," they charged. "He has Addison's disease." With that dread disease he might not live very long, they implied.

Once again Senator Kennedy went into action. His doctors issued a denial and said the only health issue was the health of our troubled economy. Many months later Mrs. Edwards wrote a letter to Mr. Kennedy apologizing for the part that she had played in making this charge.

Mr. Kennedy, of course, had a very troublesome back problem. He also had a thyroid deficiency and was taking medication to maintain a proper thyroid balance. This is a fairly common problem and not the "mysterious" or "dread" disease that it has been implied he had.

Kennedy hated to talk about his health. He took care of himself and was always "in control" of his physical as well as his emotional well-being.

As an anti-climax to all these rumors, on July 5th, Mr. Johnson announced his candidacy for the Presidency. As he left for Los Angeles he had one last blow in his pocket. Mr. Sam's "Board of Education," made up of the legislative allies of Rayburn and Johnson, had decided to recess Congress from July 2nd until the 8th of August.

Ordinarily, the Congress would adjourn *sine die* just before the convention and not meet again until after the new year when the elections were all over. Mr. Johnson no doubt calculated that he could bargain with the delegates on his ability to get legislation through the Congress. Therefore, if they would vote for him, he would go back and see that some of their pet projects were enacted. It would also show how effective he would be if he were to become President, because he would be able to work closely with his Congress. If, on the other hand, they didn't give him their votes, he could make it very difficult for them to work with Congress.

"Why Mr. Johnson, the masterminded Majority Leader, would ever dream up a scheme like this is beyond me," Mr. Kennedy said. "Even if he is the Democratic nominee, what can it possibly gain? The Republicans will do everything in their power to embarrass the Democrats."

There is one thing for sure. Mr. Johnson was not thinking about "what is good for the party"—for this decision almost cost John F. Kennedy and Lyndon Baines Johnson the election!

CHAPTER

V

The Nomination Is Assured

MR. KENNEDY had been so busy answering blasts by President Truman and issuing statements about his health, that he gave only passing notice to Mr. Johnson's announcement for the Presidency. It was really no surprise to anyone. "Don't let anyone kid you," said Mr. Kennedy. "He thinks he is going to win. Otherwise he never would have made his announcement. He is too egotistical to think anything else."

This was going to be an interesting convention!

For several months Los Angeles had been convention-conscious with the various candidates establishing headquarters from one end of the city to the other. All the headquarters were full of busy staff members catering to the whims and desires of those important people, the delegates, the so-called talent scouts. The scramble was reminiscent of the gold rush days in California in the later part of the nineteenth century. This time, however, the delegates were the gold nuggets the candidates were panning.

Kennedy's remark about Mr. Johnson's egotism was confirmed by the Texas Senator's statement on stepping off his plane at the Los Angeles airport. Johnson took one look toward the City of the Angels and exclaimed, "California, here I *am!*"

We were told by the Kennedy aides who were present that the hundred-odd people who had been milling around waiting to greet him, most of them men in ten-gallon hats, answered with whistles and shouts of YIPPEE-KI Y-I-P-P-I-E. After the shouting died down, Mr. Johnson went on to say, "It doesn't matter how many razzle-dazzle predictions you get. The only thing that's important is who ought to lead this nation." Once again there was loud whooping and hollering.

He stepped off of the platform, walked to a car that was waiting for him and soon he, his wife, Lady Bird, and his two daughters were speeding along the Freeway bound for the Biltmore Hotel. On their way to their suite on the seventh floor they stopped at the Johnson hospitality rooms. Their hard-working staff rushed up to greet them. They wandered around shaking hands with a few politicians and a sprinkling of followers who had been plunging their hands into the dozens and dozens of buckets of Austin, Texas taffy that lined the walls.

As they walked around the rooms they must have noticed—they couldn't miss it—an enormous Texas style hat, measuring six feet from brim to brim, suspended against one of the walls. "LBJ for USA" were the bold letters on the hat band. In the background over the loudspeakers throbbed the gripping strains of LBJ's theme song, "The Yellow Rose of Texas." And among all of the Johnson brochures and publicity were "yellow rose" favors for the guests.

When Mr. Kennedy arrived at the airport the next day, nearly two thousand enthusiastic greeters were on hand to meet him. As he stepped off the plane and waved to them there was squealing, jumping—utter confusion. They pushed and they shoved to get near, to touch him, as he made his way to a small platform set up for him to say a few words. This crowd was made up of teen-agers and boys and girls in their early twenties. It was too bad that they couldn't do the voting in the convention. Mr. Kennedy's worries would have vanished.

Mr. Kennedy shouted to that exuberant band of supporters: "A few days ago another candidate said that we needed a man with a little gray in his hair. We put that gray in his hair and we will continue to do so." The crowd loved his wit. And then he added, "I think we are going to win, but I don't think we have it wrapped up."

His motorcade, which inched along all the way down the Freeway, finally arrived at the Biltmore

Hotel. Like Mr. Johnson, the first thing that he did was to visit his hospitality headquarters. Once again he found enthusiastic young people handing out literature and PT-boat tie clasps. When they saw him and realized that he had arrived, they forgot what they were doing and swamped him, shoving all kinds of papers and pens at him, hoping to get his autograph. Standing crouched over, he wrote his name time after time until, finally, he straightened up, edged his way to the door and went up to his suite on the ninth floor.

I had set up an office in this suite the night before and I was eagerly waiting for Mr. Kennedy to arrive. As he traveled along the route to the suite, various people called me and reported on his progress. They would say, "Oh boy, the crowd is simply fantastic. Can you hear them yelling and screaming? The traffic is all tied up. They are all trying to get a look at Mr. Kennedy." "You should see them down here in the hospitality room. All of the other hospitality rooms are vacant. They have all come over here to get Mr. Kennedy's autograph."

Mr. Kennedy greeted me warmly and then seemed very anxious to start working. "This is going to be a busy week. Do I have any mail, any telephone calls?" he asked. We were in business. My office was the hub of an enormous wheel which began to turn faster and faster. The axle on which the wheel moved was, of course, John Kennedy. He could be found at the Beverly Hilton Hotel, the hideaway out on North Rossmore

Street, or in his suite in the Biltmore. The most important was an office located out near the Sports Arena where the convention was going to be held. In this office were the liaison men who worked around the clock in their drive to tie up every possible delegate. They, too, had a suite of offices in the Biltmore Hotel.

My work had now started. Between incessant telephone calls, I was arranging the schedule for Mr. Kennedy to attend state caucuses. The liaison men and Mr. Kennedy would make up the list of state caucuses that Mr. Kennedy should attend each day and it was up to me to call the man in charge of the caucus, make arrangements for Mr. Kennedy to appear, get the time of his appearance, and then type all of his appointments and appearances so that Pierre Salinger could put out a press release showing Mr. Kennedy's activities the next day.

Kennedy girls in red, white and blue dresses and straw hats were showing up out at the Sports Arena and so were hundreds of spirited "Draft Stevenson" volunteers. These Stevenson volunteers were not allowed into the Convention Hall, but stormed around at the entrance. "The volunteers who are showing up for Stevenson make it difficult to get any kind of assurance from him, because this has given him a glimmer of hope that he might still have a chance," I heard someone say to Mr. Kennedy. "That's true," said Mr. Kennedy, "but his strength lies only here in California." However, the Johnson press reports saw real hope in these demonstrations and in the refusal of California to swing decisively to Mr. Kennedy. John Connally was saying that the split in the California delegation meant that there was a revolt in the West, and a revolt in the Middle West. "Kennedy figures are exaggerated," the Johnson press releases stated.

Mrs. Eleanor Roosevelt also hoped that her candidate Adlai Stevenson would somehow still be nominated. She was very much opposed to Mr. Kennedy and when she learned that some of the Stevenson supporters had gone over to Mr. Kennedy she was extremely disturbed. She announced, "How can anyone accept second best until you have done all you can to get the best."

There were light moments too. Two preachers from Texas were picketing the convention, demanding that the convention reject a Catholic nominee and pass a resolution asking for separation of Church and State.

After each caucus, after each appointment, there were press releases with new counts, new predictions, more claims that more delegate votes had been added. "We'll probably get more votes on the first ballot and more on the second ballot than any other man from my area has ever received in one hundred years," Mr. Johnson told the caucuses. We had news for him. No one was ever going to know what the votes would have been on the second ballot because we were aiming to win on the first.

Mr. Johnson continued to criticize Mr. Kennedy for

his absenteeism in the Congress and what he claimed was Kennedy's mediocre legislative record. As he went from caucus to caucus he also attacked the Kennedy family. He attacked the Kennedy wealth. "I haven't had anything given to me," he told the delegates. "Whatever I have and whatever I hope to get will be because of whatever energy and talents I have."

Mr. Johnson must have begun to sense the temper of the convention because, as one Texan said, "Lyndon has lost his fast ball, his curve ball, and now he is going to use his mud ball." He attacked Mr. Kennedy's father by saying, "I wasn't any Chamberlain umbrella man."

Even though Johnson was on the seventh floor of the Biltmore Hotel and Kennedy was on the ninth, the two candidates seldom met. Their only contact were the press releases and telephone calls that flew like missiles between staff members of the two offices.

The one time they did meet was by accident outside the South Carolina caucus. I had called our South Carolina contact man to tell him that Mr. Kennedy was on his way. "Things are a little gummed up at this end," he said, "there are other candidates waiting to talk to the delegates. In fact, Mr. Johnson is waiting his turn to talk, but we will take care of Mr. Kennedy as soon as he arrives." The contact man called me back and said, "You should have been here. Mr. Johnson got so mad when he saw Mr. Kennedy that he got up out of his chair and went over to him

—poked his face right into Senator Kennedy's face and said something about this being his territory." "What did Mr. Kennedy do?" I asked. "Oh, he just smiled and sat down," was the reply.

I guess the thing that really enraged Mr. Johnson was Mr. Kennedy's telegram to the Southern delegations asking for the chance to appear before them. The telegram went to the Chairmen of the Alabama, Florida, Georgia, Kentucky, Louisiana, Mississippi, North Carolina, South Carolina, Tennessee, Texas, and Virginia delegations. It read: "I am most grateful for the support and friendship of my Southern friends in 1956. As a candidate for President, I would appeciate very much the privilege of meeting your 1960 delegation in your caucus to explain my views and to answer their questions. If this privilege can be extended to me, please telephone my personal secretary, Mrs. Evelyn Lincoln, Phone Madison 6-3592, Ext. 27. Sincerely, John F. Kennedy."

His meeting with the South Carolina delegation was a result of that telegram. The response from the Southern states was extremely gratifying to Mr. Kennedy. There was only one state that did not feel like the others and that was Texas. Mr. Johnson, sensing a chance to embarrass Mr. Kennedy, had fired back a reply to the telegram: "I am very happy to know that you are grateful for the support and friendship that your Southern friends gave you in 1956. It is interesting to know you need them now. Personally, I believe that the problems before us are far too important to be determined on the basis solely of regional and sectional issues. As a firm believer in the democratic process, especially as it relates to national party conventions, may I suggest that in response to your request we appear together before a joint session of the Texas and Massachusetts delegations in caucus and debate the major issues on which these bodies solemnly will act later this week. It would be in the interest of our party that this session be open to a free coverage by press, television, and radio. I propose that we meet at 3 o'clock on Tuesday, July 12, at a place to be determined and of which I will advise you promptly. Best regards. Sincerely, Lyndon B. Johnson."

Mr. Kennedy laughed and said, "Mr. Johnson is so sure that his big image of being the Majority Leader is going to make every one of these delegates wilt and vote for him. How ridiculous to have Massachusetts and Texas delegations meet together. All I asked was to appear before the Texas caucus. Is he afraid that I might sway them if he doesn't appear with me? After all, he is the favorite son and all of the delegates are committed to vote for him on the first ballot."

So Congressman John McCormack, Chairman of the Massachusetts delegation, rejected the invitation of a joint session, saying that it was "inconsistent with the seriousness of the convention" and "it tends to create unnecessary emotionalism."

But Johnson protested. This time his wire read: "May I earnestly urge you, Jack, to reconsider your refusal to permit your delegation to join with ours for this important discussion of issues." They finally agreed to meet in a debate before the Texas delegation in the Grand Ballroom of the Biltmore. "This should be good," my husband Abe said. "Remember what Mr. Kennedy did to Humphrey in West Virginia?" The men, both of them confident, were finally going to meet in face-to-face battle.

Here was the big chance to trap young Kennedy, the Majority Leader must have thought. Truman's blast had boomeranged. John Connally and India Edwards had failed. People were not believing that the swift-moving Massachusetts man who put in hours that would kill a horse, was about to die from adrenal deficiency. Adlai Stevenson was not doing so well. Illinois had caucused the night before and voted to give Stevenson only 2 votes, and Kennedy 59, thus sewing up that delegation which was the key to the "Stop Kennedy" effort. The very morning of the scheduled debate, Governor Lawrence of Pennsylvania, after notifying Adlai Stevenson the night before, announced that Pennsylvania would go for Mr. Kennedy on the first ballot.

Things were falling into place. It was going to be interesting to find out how Mr. Johnson thought he could maneuver himself out of the corner he was now in. It was certainly unusual for a convention to have the two leading candidates debate before the actual balloting, but then again this whole campaign had been different and unusual. Perhaps Mr. Johnson still felt that he could go before the TV cameras and settle once and for all who was the superior man in this race.

Tension ran high in our office the afternoon of the debate. My husband, Abe, is a political scientist who has taught at New Mexico University and New York University. At this time he was Administrative Assistant to Congressman Torbert H. Macdonald. He was going to be my eyes and ears at the historic confrontation. He left for the ballroom thirty minutes early to be sure that he wouldn't miss a thing. One by one others rushed out and down to the ballroom. When the hands of the clock pointed to 3:00, the scheduled time for the debate to begin, I was the only one left in the suite during the debate.

Then Abe rushed in. Once again the office had turned into a bedlam and the telephones were simply maddening. However, I stopped and listened intently to what Abe was saying. As best he could, above the commotion, he gave me the highlights of the encounter.

When he came into the ballroom it was filled with radio and television men working on equipment to be used during the debate. Every now and then a newspaperman or a radio announcer would check on lighting, space for the press, and things essential to their operation. The debate had certainly added flavor to this convention. People came in, walked around, huddled into little groups, first discussing Mr. Johnson, then Mr. Kennedy, and the effect the debate would have on the delegates.

As time went on, more and more men with ten-gallon hats showed up, but that was natural. The debate was going to be held at a caucus of the Texas delegation. Abe, however, said that it began to look like an afternoon down on the ranch. In fact, he heard one of the big boys with fancy cowboy boots say in a loud voice, "Lyndon's a fighter and a Texan never gives up. He'll show that young Kennedy who is the better man."

At the time these Texans were talking about Mr. Johnson being a fighter and a better man, Washington *Post* publisher, the late Philip Graham, in his notes written on July 19, 1960, records that Mr. Johnson had come back to his hotel suite about 2:00 o'clock after a round of caucuses. He was in such an enraged mood about the debate that his staff insisted that he go to bed. In describing this scene Mr. Graham says: "A Negro couple from his ranch were in the room throughout our lunch, and the three of us converged upon him, disrobed, pajamaed him and got him in bed." At ten minutes to three, he was still in his pajamas according to Graham. It was at this time that Mr. Graham and Mr. Johnson started to discuss the debate. Mr. Graham advised Mr. Johnson that Walter Lippman had declared for Kennedy that morning, rejecting Johnson as "an ignoramus about the world." Then, Mr. Graham said, he told Mr. Johnson that he should stay on "the high road" during the debate. Mr. Graham evidently got Mr. Johnson down to the ballroom on time because it was just about 3:00 o'clock when he appeared in the door.

As he walked down the aisle toward the platform the applause was deafening. The predominantly Texas crowd whooped and waved those big hats in the air. When Mr. Kennedy stepped up beside him, only a sprinkling of applause could be heard.

Mr. Johnson spoke first. His plea was impassioned. He ran through all of his accomplishments over the years—his great experience in the Congress, and especially the leadership he had asserted as the Majority Leader of the Senate—appealing to the TV, radio, and newsmen. He started out on "the high road." Then he started attacking Mr. Kennedy by innuendo. He told how during the filibuster fight he had answered all fifty quorum calls and was recorded in all fifty votes in the effort to break the filibuster earlier that year. "Some Senators," he said, "answered no quorum calls and missed thirty-four of the roll calls during the filibuster." He boasted that he had never voted wrong on farm questions, but "some" Senators had.

When he finished the big Texans applauded vigorously and nodded to each other as though he had won his point. Mr. Kennedy walked humbly to the front of the platform and started to talk. He seemed relaxed and there was a twinkle in his eye, Abe said. Since the Majority Leader had not specified who the Senate backsliders were, Mr. Kennedy in mock seriousness said, "I assume he was talking about some other candidate, not me. I don't think I will argue because I don't think Senator Johnson and I disagree on the great issues that face us."

"I want to commend him," Mr. Kennedy went on to say, "for a wonderful record answering these quorum calls. It was true," he continued, "I was not present at all those occasions—I was not Majority Leader."

Mr. Kennedy concluded by saying, "So I come here today full of admiration for Senator Johnson, full of affection for him, strongly in support of him—for Majority Leader."

Even the over enthusiastic Texans could not resist breaking into the spirited applause that followed Mr. Kennedy's appearance. The personal showdown was over, and the broadsword had been damaged by the rapier. The events that took place after this dramatic debate, up until the actual balloting, seemed drab in comparison.

The scene that rolled before Mr. Johnson's eyes as he sat in his hotel room watching the call of the states must have been excruciating. It probably explains why he never went out to his Convention Hall headquarters to thank his loyal supporters for the work they had done, even in defeat.

They said that he took to the bed. Speaker Rayburn, too, was tired. He sat in Convention Hall sadly watching the balloting—an unmarked tally sheet in his hand.

CHAPTER

VI

The Vice-Presidential Candidate

"WE NEED only eleven votes—eleven votes!" we all shouted as we watched the convention out in Mr. Kennedy's hideaway on North Rossmore Street. We held our breath waiting to see whether we would get those eleven votes, or whether this would be the high water mark. Others had come close in past conventions, only to lose ground steadily on later ballots, and, finally, to sink out of sight. "Look, there's Teddy with the Wyoming delegation." When the Wyoming vote was announced, we knew and the announcer knew, that the balloting was all over. John Kennedy had won. His immediate concern was to share the good news with Jackie. So he called her at Hyannis Port, Massachusetts. His next move was to go directly to the Sports Arena to thank the tired delegates.

I rode with him to the Sports Arena and later,

after a thrilling demonstration of support, back to the hideaway. As we pulled up to the door, he said, "Why don't you come in a little while, Mrs. Lincoln? You don't have to go back to the hotel yet." He was tired and glad that it was all over, and I could see that he wanted time to unwind.

There was a gay atmosphere inside the apartment. When we weren't talking over the telephone, which rang incessantly, we joked and cut up like a group of enthusiastic collegians after a thrilling game and their team had won the championship. I couldn't resist the temptation to sit down at the piano and pick out a few gleeful strains—in spite of my most limited skill. My fingers automatically started to play "When Irish Eyes are Smiling," a song that accurately described Mr. Kennedy's expression that night. "We sure gave the stick to Lyndon," Kennedy was saying as he strolled around, his shirt tail sticking out and his collar unbuttoned. Then someone asked, "Did he come to the Sports Arena to congratulate you?" "If he did, I didn't see him."

A little later Mr. Kennedy asked me, "What's my first appointment in the morning, Mrs. Lincoln?" I had learned, through many years of experience, to carry his appointment book and all of his telephone numbers with me, regardless of where we were. "Your first appointment in the morning is at eleven thirty with the southern leaders," I told him. He nodded and then went back into his bedroom. He was back in a moment. "Remind me to get in touch with Smathers in the morning," he said, and then he added, "Also, I'd like to have Lyndon at the meeting of the southern leaders. Will you call him first thing in the morning?"

First thing in the morning! It must be almost morning now, I thought. Now that it was over, I felt limp and exhausted. I said goodnight to Mr. Kennedy and left for the hotel. Before coming out to the hideaway I had left Abe in the hotel suite to answer the telephone. Now, Abe waved to me as I entered. He was busy on the telephone, but other telephones were ringing, so I gave him a hand. Between calls he said: "What took you so long?" "Long," I said. "We came as fast as we could."

"Well, Mr. Kennedy called a little while ago and asked for you," my husband reported. "He did?" I said. "Why I just left him. What did he want?" Abe said, "He wanted to dictate a wire for you to take down to Lyndon. And when he learned that you were not here, he dictated it to me!"

Abe handed me the envelope on which he had written the message that Mr. Kennedy wanted delivered to Mr. Johnson. It said, "Dear Lyndon: If it is agreeable with you, I would like to talk to you in your room tomorrow morning at 10:00 (signed) Jack."

"Did you type it up?" I asked. "Yes, and I called down to see if he was there," Abe replied. "Was he there?" I said. "The person that answered the phone said that Mr. Johnson had gone to bed and did not want to be disturbed, but if I wanted to bring the wire down, he would meet me at the door," Abe continued. So he had delivered the message.

After we left the suite to go to our hotel room we discussed all of the events that had taken place before and after the balloting. But the one thing uppermost in our minds was to get to bed and soon as our heads hit the pillows, we were asleep.

What seemed like only a minute later, but must have been around 4:30 in the morning, my telephone rang. "Mrs. Lincoln," Mr. Kennedy said, "was my message delivered to Lyndon?" My mind was clogged with sleep, but I managed to mumble, "Yes, Mr. Kennedy." Then he hurriedly asked, "Would you read it to me?" Whether he thought I had it in bed with me, I will never know. When I told him exactly what was in the wire, there was a pause, as though he were thinking.

He paused so long I almost thought he had left the phone. Then he said, "Thanks, Mrs. Lincoln." Abe sat up. "Who was that?" "Mr. Kennedy." "What did he want?" "He wanted to know if his message had been delivered to Johnson, and what was in it."

Now I could tell Abe was beginning to wonder if he had made a mistake in taking down the message, because he said, "Was he mad when you told him?" "No," I said, "he seemed puzzled, and I heard him say to someone, 'I should have mentioned the southern leaders' meeting.' Then he hung up."

In putting together all of the little bits and pieces

surrounding what took place that night following the balloting, it might be well to remember that Philip Graham, a very close friend of Mr. Johnson, had for a long time been extremely interested in Mr. Johnson's candidacy for the Presidency. However, after all of the candidates had gathered at Los Angeles for the convention, it didn't take long for him to realize that Mr. Kennedy might win on the very first ballot. Mr. Graham was a constant visitor to the Johnson suite. He must have discussed the Vice Presidency with Mr. Johnson because he sent news items to his paper indicating that Mr. Kennedy was considering giving the Vice Presidency to Mr. Johnson if he was nominated. In fact, the news story appeared on the front page of his paper on Monday, July 11th, the day the convention opened. The item said, "The word here tonight is that Senator John F. Kennedy will offer the Vice Presidential nomination to Senate Majority Leader Lyndon B. Johnson." As a smart newspaper man, Mr. Graham must have known that sometimes, a prediction, even an unlikely one, helps make things come true.

Graham followed this up with another item which he sent to his paper the night of Kennedy's nomination. "There is no reason to doubt that Senator Kennedy's own personal preference is to offer the Vice Presidential nomination to Senate Majority Leader Lyndon B. Johnson."

However, there was *never* any talk in the office that

Mr. Johnson was to be the running-mate. I would certainly have heard something of it if there had been. Stuart Symington and Henry Jackson were mentioned importantly, but, it seemed to me, Orville Freeman was the front-runner in conversations as to who would be the best candidate if Mr. Kennedy got the nomination.

The groundwork had been laid. When the wire Abe had written out arrived in the Johnson suite, stating that Mr. Kennedy wanted to see him in the morning at 10:00 A.M., the next step was to link this wire with the idea that he was coming down there to offer Mr. Johnson the Vice Presidency.

This disturbing rumor must have reached Mr. Kennedy. Otherwise, he never would have called me to find out what was in that wire. If Mr. Kennedy really had been considering putting Mr. Johnson on the ticket with him before this, the atmosphere around the suite in the Biltmore that next morning would have been different.

In fact, I am sure that the 10:00 meeting Mr. Kennedy requested in that telegram was meant only to give Mr. Kennedy a chance to gracefully shake Johnson's hand after his defeat and to discuss with him the southern leaders' meeting scheduled for later that day. There is no doubt in my mind about it. Mr. Kennedy did *not* plan to offer Johnson the Vice-Presidential nomination at the time the telegram was sent.

What should have been a great time to slap backs

and bask in the limelight of a great victory turned out instead to be a morning filled with confusion and long faces. Everyone coming in looked glum. The one question they all seemed to ask was, "How can anyone who has been so opposed to everything we have been doing possibly want to join us?"

Still, Mr. Kennedy undoubtedly felt that since these news leaks had occurred, it was essential that he offer the nomination to Mr. Johnson to avoid publicly slighting the Senate Majority Leader. If the story that Johnson would be chosen had not been so prominently placed, it might have been possible to avoid asking him, but now, it seemed necessary to make the gesture.

Mr. Kennedy and Bob were in the bedroom talking very intently. Mr. Kennedy went to get a drink of water and his brother sat glumly on the bed. I came in with some messages and looked from one to the other.

Then, Bob said to Mr. Kennedy, "Are you sure you want to do this?"

He answered "Yes" and Bob put in the call to the Johnson suite to say that Mr. Kennedy would be down to see him—at 10:00 o'clock, the time he had asked to see him. He was told that Mr. Johnson was in bed, but would be available in about ten minutes. Before Bob had hung up the receiver, the Johnson people spread the word to the reporters that Mr. Kennedy was on his way down to offer the Vice Presidency to Mr. Johnson. When I asked some of the reporters who were calling to find out if this was true, how they knew that he was going down there, they told me that Walter Jenkins and Bobby Baker, who were in the Johnson suite, had told them.

Mr. Kennedy did not know of this latest news leak because he came out into my office and said to me, "I am going down now." I said to him, "Do you think he will accept?" "No, I don't," he replied. Then he slipped out of the door as quietly and quickly as possible. He told me that he was going to walk down the two flights of stairs so that he would not be noticed. What a surprise it must have been to him when he saw that huge crowd of newspaper reporters and cameramen waiting for him.

Mr. Kennedy returned a few minutes later and as he shot through the door I could see from the expression on his face that he was not pleased at the outcome. I followed Mr. Kennedy into that room as quickly as I could and I learned that Mr. Johnson had accepted the offer, but in his own characteristic way. What he actually did was to express an "interest" in the offer, thereby shutting the door on anyone else getting it or being considered. Unlike others who would have given their eye teeth to be asked and would have given immediate acceptance, Mr. Johnson stalled for time, as though this was something that he had never expected. He said he wanted to check with various people before making a final decision. He also wanted it to appear that Mr. Kennedy had walked down those two flights of stairs and had begged him to accept.

In examining some of the evidence that "turns up"

now and then to substantiate Mr. Johnson's version of how he was chosen, there are many loopholes, many inaccuracies. Much reliance has been placed on notes written by the late Philip Graham. The notes, incidentally, were dated July 19, 1960—several days after the convention—and were not published until after his death.

In his notes Mr. Graham states that, "In the course of the day [Monday, July 11th] Joe Alsop and I began discussing the merit of Johnson as a running-mate. At Joe's urging, I accompanied him to Kennedy's suite on the 9th floor of the Biltmore where, after considerable delay (and after much observation of the hubbub in what Joe termed 'the antechambers of history') Kennedy appeared and we went with him into a living room for the five minutes we had asked for."

According to my diary for that day, those two men *did not* see Mr. Kennedy in his suite. I was in the suite all day and it is not possible that I could have missed them. Joe Alsop did, however, have a five-minute appointment with Mr. Kennedy on *Sunday*, July 10, 1960 at 6:00 P.M. I was in the living room at the time of that appointment because I was helping a cameraman set up his equipment and I overheard the conversation which consisted of discussing what Mr. Kennedy thought his chances were for winning the Presidential nomination.

The following sentence from Graham's account is

therefore complete fiction. Graham wrote, "At Joe's request, I did the greatest portion of our talking and urged Kennedy to offer the Vice Presidency to Johnson. He immediately agreed, so immediately as to leave me doubting the easy triumph . . ."

I might add that in my twelve years with John Kennedy I had never seen him agree immediately to anything as important as this. On some minor problem he might have agreed, but on a situation like this, he would certainly think carefully and consult other people before acting.

Also, on Monday, July 11th, the Kennedy forces were preparing telegrams to be sent to southern leaders asking if Mr. Kennedy could appear at their caucuses. His mind was entirely absorbed with getting nominated and getting delegates lined up for his Presidential candidacy. Picking a Vice President was premature. And John Kennedy always concentrated his energies. He took first things first and moved ahead carefully, considering one step at a time.

All during the convention, Mr. Kennedy had let a considerable number of men know that if he were nominated he would most certainly consider them for his running-mate. This is standard convention politics and "consider" is a usefully vague word. That was why men like Governor Orville Freeman, Senator Stuart Symington, and Senator Henry "Scoop" Jackson were always prominently mentioned. He also wanted the good will of the Majority Leader, not only when they returned to the rump session of Congress, but to help bring Texas back into the Democratic column in November.

Mr. Graham, in his convention notes, added that before the nomination, on Tuesday, July 12, "by clerical error, the Kennedy staff had sent to the Texas delegation a form telegram they were sending to all delegations. It was signed by Kennedy and asked for a chance to meet with the delegation."

I typed out that telegram to the Texas delegation and to all the other southern delegations, and I know that it was not a clerical error, but a shrewd maneuver by Mr. Kennedy to show he conceded nothing to Mr. Johnson, even his home state, and that he was not afraid to challenge him on hostile ground.

Graham said that on July 13, "at 5:00 A.M. Wednesday, I got a wild idea and wrote it out. It consisted of a message to the Convention from Kennedy, to be read by Stevenson on Thursday, asking the delegates to draft Johnson for VP." He said he discussed this idea with Mr. Kennedy saying he had some longhand scribble he could leave with Sorensen or Bobby. To which Kennedy supposedly said, "Leave it with me only." Then Graham said he had it typed and left it with "Mrs. Lincoln." My notes are very complete for this period, and I do not remember receiving an envelope from Mr. Graham.

At the time Mr. Graham was writing to his paper that Mr. Kennedy's personal preference was to offer the Vice-Presidential nomination to Mr. Johnson, another influential writer and friend of Mr. Johnson since the Roosevelt days, Joe Alsop, who, like Mr. Graham, his boss, was in favor of a Kennedy-Johnson ticket, wrote an article published the day of Kennedy's nomination which said, "A Democratic ticket composed of John F. Kennedy of Massachusetts and Lyndon B. Johnson of Texas in the second spot cannot be absolutely ruled out, despite the almost universal assumption to the contrary."

It has been said that Bobby Baker had talked of a dream ticket of Johnson–Kennedy, and his next choice would be Kennedy–Johnson. Of course, Mr. Kennedy was dead set against being second man on any ticket. "It's first place or nothing," he said. "No matter what anybody says we won't take second place. Nobody's going to make a deal with us in a back room somewhere for second place on the ticket."

Another confidential note was unearthed by a friend of former Vice President John N. Garner, Lawrence W. "Chip" Roberts. This note was so confidential that only Mr. Roberts, Mr. Garner, and Mr. Johnson knew about it. Ninety-one-year-old Garner, it seems, was riding in a car. He happened to glance up and saw his old friend, Chip Roberts, and his wife going by in a train. Garner is said to have signaled them frantically so that he could give Roberts a message to take with him to the convention. He shouted and Mrs. Roberts took down the following: "I want you to take this message confidentially and at once to Sam and Lyndon. . . . As you know," Garner bellowed on, "I love Old Sam and I'm one hundred percent for Lyndon. . . . I am firmly convinced the boy will be nominated on the very first roll call, and you have to be prepared to act fast."

"As sure as gun's iron," Garner said, Kennedy would offer Johnson the number two spot knowing he needed him to win. "I urge you to play your cards close to your chest and wait for the boy to make the approach—which I'm sure he will—and Lyndon must be ready to accept."

Garner also said he himself had taken the second spot with a younger Presidential candidate, and it hadn't hurt him any. As a persuasive clincher, he reportedly urged that Lady Bird was a smart politician who would rather have Lyndon "take it easy" as Vice President than keep at the grind of Majority Leader.

All of this sage advice supposedly came from a man who at one time had said that the Vice Presidency wasn't worth "a warm bucket of spit." Another puzzling thing is that Mr. Johnson was supposed to be putting in a call to Mr. Garner to ask his advice. However, if he had this long memorandum rescued from a speeding train, it would seem that a telephone call would be unnecessary.

Lady Bird also added her version. "It was certainly the most dramatic and emotion-laden day in our lives. I was surprised when the Senator called and asked

Lyndon to go on the ticket as his running-mate." (I have no record of any such call.)

She was surprised, she added, "Because they are very different people, but I think it was a very independent and wonderful decision on the part of Senator Kennedy, and with the intention of unifying the country and the party, and I am mighty proud that Lyndon made the decision he did."

Her husband, she reflected three months later, ". . . tried just as hard as he could for the top spot and not having gotten that—eight hundred of the delegates chose Kennedy, four hundred chose him—then his choice was simple. 'Shall I just,' as he expressed it, 'pick up my marbles and go home? Or shall I throw in my experience and ability, and my worth, whatever it is, in the job I am asked to do?' "

While Mr. Johnson was consulting all his advisors, Mr. Kennedy was sounding out the acceptability of a Kennedy–Johnson ticket. He learned that many of the old-line big city politicians would go along with Mr. Johnson because they felt he was a real pol whose methods they understood. Southern support could pretty much be taken for granted, from both the segregationist and moderate wings. But the labor leaders were furious. They were opposed to having a candidate from a right-to-work law state, who had voted to override the vetoes of two Democratic Presidents. Texas Governor Price Daniel was described as being "shocked and jarred back to his Texas ancestors" over the idea that Johnson would consent to run with Kennedy.

Governor G. Mennen Williams told his delegates: "This is preposterous. After our remarkable achievement in obtaining the civil rights plank in the platform, it is like stepping down from the clouds. For some of us, the suggestion was catastrophic and we have made it known in no uncertain terms."

Senator William Proxmire tried to mollify his Wisconsin delegation caucus by saying that Mr. Johnson would do the liberal Democratic cause less damage in the Vice President's chair than in the Majority Leader's office. However, leaders of New York's influential Liberal Party threatened to withhold a place on their ballot for Mr. Kennedy if Lyndon Johnson's name had to go on the ballot too.

Joseph Rauh of the District of Columbia delegation, upon hearing the news, shouted over television, "Say it isn't so, Jack." The clamor grew so loud that afternoon that Bob Kennedy was sent by his brother to the Johnson suite to advise him of the opposition that was brewing. Mr. Kennedy also instructed Bob to ask Johnson to consider taking over the Chairmanship of the Democratic National Committee instead of the Vice-Presidential nomination. It might have been at this point that Mr. Johnson developed a livid dislike for Bob Kennedy, although some thought that the bad blood between them had deeper roots. In any event, Bob had come to the Johnson suite at the request of his brother and to inform Mr. Johnson of the trouble that the suggestion of his name was causing. Mr. Johnson might have assumed that this "young squirt" was trying on his own to dump him from the ticket. This was not so. In fact, Bob never got the chance to suggest the National Committee Chairmanship.

There was a great deal of disappointment among the men from the Midwest and the West when they learned that Mr. Johnson was going to be the nominee. They took their disappointment very well, although they knew they would never get the chance to prove what they might have done for Mr. Kennedy in the states of their region had they been on the ticket. They knew writers would always speak of the electoral votes Mr. Johnson had brought Mr. Kennedy in the South, with little notice of the lost votes *they* might have helped win for him in the Midwest or the West.

Mr. Johnson finally accepted, and Mr. Kennedy made the announcement at 4:00 P.M. It was brief and direct. Immediately, Mr. Johnson came out of the confusion of his suite. The words that he uttered were typical of the atmosphere that he had created and his natural instinct for showmanship.

"When Senator Kennedy walked down three [*sic*] flights of stairs to ask me to be his running mate, I could not say no."

CHAPTER VII

A Rough Rump Session

ALMOST FORGOTTEN in the excitement of getting ready for the challenging campaign against Mr. Nixon was the little left-over strategy that Rayburn and Johnson had thought would get the Presidential nomination for Mr. Johnson—the rump session of Congress. The strategy didn't work, but the rump session remained and they still had to come back to the United States Senate to work on legislation for three weeks, starting August 8th.

This little time bomb was going to test the newly formed partnership between Mr. Kennedy and Mr. Johnson in a very curious way. As columnist George Dixon remarked, "I never thought I'd live to see the upside down day when the senior Senator from Texas would be under the junior Senator from Massachusetts and I only hope they can stay in the reversed positions without the blood running to their heads. . . . If it works," he added, "this will be the greatest acrobatic feat in history." It was like a play in which everybody changes roles during intermission.

Of course, there were others who had a big stake in the failure or success, smoothness or turmoil, of this rump session. Since it was an election year, all of the Congressmen, together with one third of the Senators, were up for election. To say that they were not anxious to get tied down in Washington would be a major understatement. They wanted to get out of hot sticky Washington and back to their districts and states to campaign. Above all they didn't want lengthy debates and roll call votes on controversial legislation.

Mr. Kennedy's uppermost thoughts in between the convention and the rump session were concentrated on the campaign against Richard Nixon, a fight that he knew was going to be difficult. He spent this time in Hyannis Port, Massachusetts holding strategy meetings with staff members, going over schedules, and making plans for the big push. Toward the end of the strategy meetings, Mr. Johnson was invited up to Hyannis where he was briefed on what they had been considering. He was upset that they hadn't brought him in from the beginning, but as Abe said, "He has been in the driver's seat so long that it is difficult for him to ride in the back."

Although the Democrats seemed to be happy with their ticket when the rump session began, they weren't happy about their presence on Capitol Hill. The Republicans, on the other hand, were jubilant. They planned to use this session to get ammunition for later in the campaign. Everyone knew it was going to be a battle, but the Democrats hoped Mr. Johnson could use his renowned strategical power to pass some worthwhile legislation—for after all that was his greatest asset.

Shortly before Mr. Kennedy left Hyannis, he had asked that we find an office near the floor of the Senate where he could talk with his staff members, meet with leaders, and hold conferences. He expected to work out of this office, as well as the main one in the Senate Office Building. Ted Reardon, Mr. Kennedy's pleasing, good natured Administrative Assistant, who had been Joe, Jr.'s roommate at Harvard, talked about it to easy going, but sometimes caustic, Joe Duke, the Senate Sergeant at Arms. Duke had a room in his suite of offices that Mr. Kennedy could use, a staff office with the usual conference table. Over in one corner was a desk with a telephone. In another corner was a little room with a refrigerator and sink where Mr. Duke stored drinks and food for visiting Senators and their guests.

The day before Mr. Kennedy returned to Washington he called me from New York and asked me to call Lyndon Johnson, Senator "Scoop" Jackson and Matt McCloskey, treasurer of the Democratic National Committee, and tell them that he would like to meet with them in his office in the Senate Office Building at 9:30 the next morning.

Scoop Jackson came first. He stopped at my desk to say good morning. We walked slowly into Mr. Kennedy's office and while he was looking at the pictures on the wall, I told Ted Sorensen that he had arrived. Ted said, "Good, I would like to talk to him." Next came burly Matt McCloskey, that big Pennsylvania contractor. He, like Senator Jackson, had laughing eyes and a jolly smile. He joined Scoop and Ted in Mr. Kennedy's office.

Then Mr. Kennedy came in. He looked fresh and tan from his stay at the Cape and he rushed into the office with gusto and full of instructions. "Are they here?" he said. "All but Lyndon Johnson," I replied. "If he doesn't show up soon, call his office and remind him that we are meeting," Mr. Kennedy said as he stepped into his office. I waited a few minutes and, just as I started to call Mr. Johnson's office, he arrived. He rushed in, as though he had just finished some big conference and had just settled very important business. "Where's the meeting?" he said. He was breathing heavily as though he had raced down the corridor. I started to get up to open the door of Mr. Kennedy's office when Mr. Kennedy came out, no doubt to give me some instructions. He said, "Hello Lyndon," and Johnson replied, "Hi'ya Jack. Sorry I'm late. I got hung up on a long distance telephone call."

At this meeting, the participants discussed proposed

plans of operation for the Congressional rump session and a tentative campaign schedule after adjournment. A joint statement was issued that day which read:

"We have discussed the legislative program for the forthcoming session. The agenda is long. The unfinished business covers a wide range of fields—all of them of key importance to the American people. There are such key issues already on the calendar as medical care for the aged, housing, aid to education, mutual security appropriations, and minimum wage legislation. We intend to devote our full energies to the enactment of this program and we will leave our principal campaigning until the end of the session. We hope to have the cooperation of the Republicans and their candidate in the enactment of this program. The short three-week period will not allow for partisanship. The American people will be quick to spot obstructionist tactics aimed at keeping us from enacting much of this legislation."

I know that those who attended that meeting were hopeful that the session would go along smoothly, but the ink was hardly dry on this statement before things started to pop. Shrewd old Senator Everett Dirksen of Illinois, with whom Lyndon Johnson had always played footsy, certainly had no part in the drafting of the words about Republican cooperation, because he quickly introduced a bill designed to open up old Democratic wounds, drive a wedge between Kennedy and Johnson, anger the conservatives, dismay the liberals, and win friends and votes for the Republicans. All of this would be accomplished with one particular kind of legislation—a civil rights bill. And that's precisely the bill that Senator Dirksen produced. It incorporated planks from both of the party platforms.

"This will be disastrous to our party," Mr. Kennedy said. Certainly this was not the time to have an open break between northern and southern Democratic Senators. "We don't want the sorry spectacle of this session being stopped at the start by a southern Democratic filibuster," Mr. Kennedy added. The Democratic leadership called a meeting and out of the huddle came the suggestion from the liberal Senator Joseph S. Clark of Pennsylvania to move to shelve this civil rights bill. The Dirksen proposal was killed by a vote of 54 to 28.

Mr. Kennedy stormed off the floor and over to his office. He felt caught in a trap and he knew what the liberals were going to say to him and about him. He remembered what the liberals had told him in Los Angeles. They had said that exactly this would happen if Mr. Johnson were on the ticket.

Mr. Kennedy called some of the liberal leaders. He tried to tell them that it was a matter of a timetable and that other legislation, which was pending, should get priority before the fight on the civil rights began. They weren't convinced at all. They said, if that is the case, he should have made a statement to that effect at the time of the vote to reduce the impact of tabling the motion. To them that motion made it look like the civil rights bill was killed for the session.

Mr. Kennedy paced up and down through his offices like a caged lion repeating that all of this embarrassment could have been avoided if only Congress could have adjourned *sine die.* "I can't understand what Lyndon was thinking about," Mr. Kennedy said, as he walked through the door.

Mr. Kennedy took a blasting the next day in the papers. They were full of statements like, "Was it, after all, a Johnson–Kennedy ticket?" "Is Johnson the master of Kennedy's House?" and "With a grin of delight on his face, Johnson forced the Republicans to a quick vote . . . After a brief conference with Johnson, Senator Kennedy (Mass.), the Democratic Presidential nominee, added a soft-voiced 'aye' to support the Clark motion."

Mr. Kennedy's Irish temper was up. He was furious over the suggestion that he was not the leader. After he read those articles in the newspapers, he said to me, "Mrs. Lincoln, bring your things and come over to the Capitol from the Senate Office Building. From now on we are going to work over there." Leaving a trail of dropped pencils, note pads, and other office paraphernalia behind, I raced along after him to the Capitol.

The first thing I noticed was that we were right across the hall from the office Mr. Johnson had as Senate Majority Leader, at the Capitol. When I mentioned this to Mr. Duke he remarked, "Oh, yes, he uses this office quite a bit." I soon learned that was an understatement, because he practically lived in the office.

There wasn't much space in that conference room for a secretary. However, we finally wedged a small table between two window ledges and every time I looked up, I saw my own face in the mirror that hung there. I was reminded of a story my father, J. N. Norton, used to tell when he was campaigning for Congress in Nebraska. It seemed that a backwoods mountaineer one day found a mirror which a tourist had lost. "Well, if it ain't my old dad," he said as he looked in the mirror. "I never knowed he had his pitcher took." He took the mirror home and stole into the attic to hide it. But his actions didn't escape his suspicious wife. That night while he slept she slipped up to the attic and found the mirror. "Hum-um," she said, looking into it, "so that's the old hag he's been chasin'." For me, as time went on, the mirror proved to be tremendously helpful. All I had to do was to look up and I could see everything that was going on behind me. And there was plenty.

Telephones were piled on this tiny table with just enough space left for me to scratch little notes. As soon as the phones were connected they started to ring, and from that moment on, they never stopped. The notes kept piling higher and higher.

There was still a lot of smoke from the civil rights hand grenade that Senator Dirksen had tossed into the

Senate. Mr. Kennedy made statements, got up petitions, held press conferences. He did everything he could think of to try to counteract the shelving of that civil rights bill.

The gleeful Republicans were having the time of their life. Now President Eisenhower entered the scene. Taking Senator Kennedy at his word about "getting America moving" he sent to the Congress a long list of proposals. Even Sam Rayburn was shocked when he saw them. He shook his head and remarked, "It would take Congress from now until Christmas to pass all this legislation. . . . I was utterly amazed."

People and events were beginning to close in on us. Never have I seen so much pressure in my whole life. It seemed that everyone in the whole country wanted to get in to see Mr. Kennedy. Somehow it doesn't take long for people to learn the listed or unlisted telephone numbers of a Presidential nominee. And those telephones, which should have been open for the members of his staff, were jammed constantly.

Much as I wanted to, I didn't have the time to run across the hall to see Mr. Johnson's office. I was told that it was very plush, with push buttons, pretty girls, and ankle deep carpeting. Everything by Johnson custom was stamped or engraved with his cattle brand, "LBJ."

The corridors of the Capitol were always filled with tourists and curious well-wishers who, whenever Mr. Kennedy was there, would hop on him like a bunch of hens after a June bug. "Will you sign this book for me, Mr. Kennedy," I would hear them say over and over again. Ordinarily Mr. Kennedy didn't mind signing all kinds of little bits of papers, books or whatnot. But right now he was anxious to get the idea across that he was the leader and so his mind was busy planning strategy while he was autographing everything imaginable.

"Mrs. Lincoln," he would say as he darted for the door, "tell everyone who calls that I am over on the floor managing a bill." Or, if he was in the office and was too busy to talk, he would say, "Tell them that I just came off the floor—must return. I will be in touch."

Our sanctuary, our office, was turning into a madhouse. In fact, it was beginning to look like one of LBJ's Texas barbecues, including the smoke. Congressmen wanted pictures taken with Mr. Kennedy for their campaigns. Organizations and groups from every state in the Union wanted an interview with Mr. Kennedy. And as these Congressmen, organizations, and groups filed in and out of our office, so did Mr. Johnson. He spent as much time in our office as he did in both his own office and on the Senate floor put together.

Every morning, there he was. "Where's Jack?" he would say. If "Jack" was there he would barge right in and start talking—never stopping. If someone else was already with Mr. Kennedy, he would stand at the door so long that it would be impolite not to ask him to join the conversation. And if he came in, once again he would start to talk. Even when he wasn't *in* our office, some member of his staff would come over or call me on the phone periodically to find out if Mr. Kennedy was looking for him. Four years of this could be maddening, I thought. Thank goodness he wouldn't have an office across the hall if Mr. Kennedy won the election.

I didn't have time to do too much typing, but I did get out some wires to the southern governors. Kennedy and Johnson had decided to hold a series of meetings with these governors, and the wires went out saying, "Could you come to Washington to meet with me and Lyndon?" The response was excellent—but to fit them all in, into an already crowded schedule, took some maneuvering.

Besides meetings like this, Mr. Kennedy had other things to do. He went to the meetings the Subcommittee on Labor was holding on *situs* picketing. There were hearings also before the Foreign Relations Committee. There were interviews with reporters; a breakfast date with James Patton, President of the Farmers Union; lunch with Adlai Stevenson and a planned trip to New York to attend a memorial meeting at Hyde Park—a meeting which marked twenty-five years since the signing of the Social Security Act.

Mr. Kennedy also had a long talk at this time with personable Terry Sanford, the soft-spoken Democratic nominee for Governor of North Carolina. Sanford had accompanied Senator Everett Jordan and Bert Bennett for an appointment with Mr. Kennedy at 4:30 P.M. on August 17th. Before the meeting broke up they discussed a luncheon for North Carolina newsmen scheduled to be held in the Supreme Court room of the Capitol with Mr. Kennedy the following week. Mr. Sanford had the distinction of being for Mr. Kennedy long before the Wisconsin primaries.

The Friday of that first week and the day before Mr. Kennedy was going to Hyde Park to attend that memorial meeting, things were really hectic! Mr. Johnson had been in and out so many times that I had lost count. His dropping in wasn't so bad, but every time he did, he would try to take over. Again and again I would hear him say, "But now let me tell you, Jack." Mr. Kennedy's fingers would begin to drum on the desk. Soon he would stand up, or would sit with the muscles in his jaws quivering—a sign to me that he was trying his best to keep from losing his temper. Finally, he blurted out in a rather stern voice, "Lyndon, instead of doing all of this talking, let's get some of this legislation moving." Mr. Johnson stormed out of the room, banging the door behind him.

That evening I noticed that Mr. Kennedy had a huskiness in his voice, but having learned a long time before not to ask him how he felt, I didn't say anything. He never wanted to discuss illness. However, the next morning when he came in before leaving for New York, he asked me to set up an appointment with a throat doctor. I thought at the time that his throat sounded better, but it might be a good idea to have it checked.

He went to New York, up to Hyde Park and then down to Newport, Rhode Island to see Mrs. Kennedy and Caroline. When he came into the office the following Monday morning he wasn't using his voice at all. He was going along with the doctor's orders that he should save his voice for a while, give it a rest. Once in a while he would forget, and although it was husky, I didn't think it sounded too bad. But most of the time he wrote messages on little pink pads. He wrote these little notes to everyone who came into the office, even to me.

Monday and Tuesday were just as hectic as Friday. And the pressure was really mounting. What was really bringing the tension was the fact that bill after bill was either stopped dead or hacked to pieces by a coalition of Republicans and conservative southern Democrats. Now people were beginning to say, "What has happened to the Democratic leadership?" And "This proves that Kennedy is really too young—too inexperienced to be President. He can't even get one bill through Congress, what would he do as President?"

Tuesday afternoon the roof fell in. Mr. Kennedy went all to pieces. What little voice he had was gone . . . gone entirely. Here he was just about to go out in a campaign that was not going to be easy, and he had no voice. The more he thought of it, the tighter his throat became. "In some ways," I said at the time, "it would have been better if he'd lost his temper. Situations like this cause heart attacks and ulcers. But he's lost his voice."

A throat specialist was called to see him that evening and Mr. Kennedy was reassured that there was nothing radically wrong with his throat and that, in time, he would get his voice back. After that, he became resigned to the situation. In fact, it seemed to me that he was relieved. He no longer had to hold back his tongue or hold back his temper. The whole burden of pushing legislation through was dumped right into Mr. Johnson's lap, because Mr. Kennedy was unable to talk to the individual Senators. Certainly he couldn't stand on the floor of the Senate arguing point by point the merits of the bill under consideration. Now they were going to have to rise or fall on the efforts of the Majority Leader.

Mr. Johnson, however, hadn't lost his voice, and he was really using it. It seemed louder than ever as he snapped orders to people around him. During those three weeks, members of his staff complained about the way he treated them. They told me how cross and cantankerous he was.

It was still nerve-racking in our office, but things had taken a different slant now that Mr. Kennedy was literally speechless. About all he could do was to smile, give a little nod, and grab for a pink pad anytime he met anyone. This pink pad system might have worked better if it hadn't been for the fact that Mr. Kennedy's handwriting was almost illegible. He could read it—and after years of struggling with it so could I—but others were not so fortunate. Mr. Johnson might have had difficulty reading the notes, because he didn't come in and out of the office as much anymore.

Nor were they using pink pads over on the floor of the Senate. There was a great deal of talking in that "do nothing" Congress. They talked about everything but what they should have been talking about, legislation. "What fool things that man has written during this session," I heard someone say. "You mean a reporter?" he was asked. "No, the Senate recorder."

The final blow came when two of Mr. Kennedy's most cherished bills, the minimum wage extension and the school aid bill, went down the drain. The session was just about over, with its major product bickering and disunity. There was only one good thing about the last day of this session—it closed the book on what will probably be recorded as one of the strangest, most hectic and futile events in congressional history.

CHAPTER

VIII

The Campaign in Dixie

THE "DO NOTHING" session was over! The atmosphere which so recently had been filled with confusion and frayed tempers suddenly changed. Now it was exciting. Even Mr. Kennedy had a new bounce in his step as he rushed into the office with last minute instructions. There was no doubt in my mind, nor I am sure, in anyone else's (except perhaps Lyndon Johnson's) that from that moment on he was going to be in charge of the Kennedy-Johnson relationship.

Throughout all of the friction and frustration which had delayed the campaign, Kennedy men and Mr. Kennedy himself had feverishly been working on organizational methods to be used in the coming weeks. "Let me see, Mrs. Lincoln," he said, "where are all the papers I will need for this meeting tonight." A meeting of speechwriters was to be held in his home in Georgetown. "In your brief case," I answered. In a few moments Mr. Kennedy with his brief case and able assistant, Ted Sorensen, started to leave. "I'll be talking to you," he called to me over his shoulder, as he opened the door. In the doorway was the silhouetted figure of Mr. Johnson, slightly turned toward his office. In a low voice I heard Mr. Kennedy say, "See you in Texas, Lyndon." Then the door closed.

Texas! Since the turn of the century only three times had Texas voted anything but Democratic. The first time was in 1928 when Catholicism and prohibition gave Herbert Hoover the slim margin of 26,000 votes in his race against the man with the derby from the sidewalks of New York—Al Smith. The other two times were in 1952 and 1956 when liberal, eloquent Adlai Stevenson ran against Dwight D. Eisenhower, a great military hero who talked peace. Ike won by over 53 percent of the votes.

This time, however, the Democrats were optimistic about Texas. The Kennedy strategists felt that Kennedy was a stronger candidate than Adlai Stevenson; Texas was the home state of Mr. Johnson; Richard M. Nixon was not Dwight D. Eisenhower, and Texans knew where their wells were oiled—in Washington.

These same strategists reasoned that if Nixon carried Texas in November it would be because he had been able to sell the voters a warmed-over Eisenhower peace issue and because he would also benefit from their powerful and deep-rooted religious prejudice against having a Catholic as President.

After they left Washington, Mr. Kennedy struck out

on a tour of the West Coast, while Mr. Johnson invaded Massachusetts. Mr. Kennedy's pattern of campaigning was the straightforward setting forth of plans and ideas for getting this country moving again. His greatest appeal was to the youth and soon there appeared at every stop, every turn of the road, the "squealers," the "jumpers," and "bouncers." He also talked to the leaders along the way, as well as to the men in the organizations that had been set up during the rustling for delegates.

On the other hand, Mr. Johnson campaigned everywhere in the same style he used down in Texas. He kissed babies, he slapped backs, he hugged the women and he was unpredictable. As his motorcade moved along the streets of Boston he noticed a mounted police officer directing traffic. Like a flash, he was out of his car asking the police officer if he would step down. To show his agility in mounting a horse he grabbed the horn of the saddle, placed his foot in the stirrup and, with great speed, threw his big frame astride the horse. Sitting in the saddle, he began to talk to the crowd—about our foreign policy!

Mr. Johnson had been very well-received in Boston. I was told by members of the press that the turnout was much bigger than he had expected. Of course he was pleased because the size of an audience was one of his greatest concerns.

The campaign trails of the two candidates were scheduled to meet in El Paso, Texas on the night of

September 11th. This was the night before Mr. Kennedy was going to appear before the Greater Houston Ministerial Association, where he would meet the religious question head on.

I don't know whether it was the turnout for Mr. Kennedy down there in El Paso on the eleventh—a turnout which was much bigger and more enthusiastic than the one for Johnson in Boston—or whether it was the lateness of the hour, or the fact that Mr. Kennedy did not want him to be on the platform with him when he met the ministers, but I got reports from our advance men that Mr. Johnson was extremely upset when Mr. Kennedy finally arrived. He was so perturbed and made such a big fuss that Mr. Kennedy said to him, "Take it easy, Lyndon, it's a long time until the eighth of November."

Mr. Kennedy had long ago learned that Mr. Johnson was extremely sensitive and thin-skinned and he tried not to upset him. Sometimes, however, it could not be helped. The crowds that had come out to meet him on his tour of the West Coast were so large and enthusiastic that it was impossible for him to maintain a strict time schedule, and there were times when Mr. Kennedy's decisions did not coincide with the ones held by Mr. Johnson.

There was still a trace of hurt feelings when they met at a breakfast in the Cortez Hotel the next morning. When he introduced Mr. Kennedy he spoke very briefly. Mr. Kennedy brushed this off lightly by turning to Mr. Johnson saying, "I was just relaxing to hear

Lyndon Johnson make a fifteen to twenty minute speech here this morning. I can see it will be a hard day for me."

Only two ministers sat on the platform with Mr. Kennedy as he appeared before the Greater Houston Ministerial Association meeting in the ballroom of the Rice Hotel. This was a battle Mr. Kennedy wanted to fight all alone. Mr. Johnson was not on the platform.

Mr. Kennedy might have been unknown in Texas when he flew into Houston at 5:15 P.M. on September 12, 1960, but when he left Houston around midnight that same night, there was no doubt that he had made a tremendous impression on a great number of people —not only in Texas but in other parts of the country.

One observer said: "The world's ablest reporters never could have duplicated on paper the emotional and human electricity that a viewer could feel in personally watching the ministers put their inquiries to Mr. Kennedy after he had finished his speech before the Greater Houston Ministerial Association. The introductions of Mr. Kennedy, the faces of members of the audience, the expressions of the questioners and the response to the answers made for a genuine sense of participation in a moment of actuality."

Speaker Sam Rayburn, who accompanied Mr. Kennedy and Mr. Johnson on their swing around Texas, must have felt the impact, because when he was asked what he thought of the speech he said, "He ate 'em raw."

Though Kennedy had stilled religious prejudice,

the smoldering feud between the various quarreling factions of Texas politics had by no means been stifled; for the moment it had been shoved under the rug. Out of courtesy, United States Senator Ralph Yarborough had been invited to accompany the candidates during their tour of Texas. However, Yarborough was still smarting from the snubs that he had received from the Johnson forces when they were making plans for the convention at Los Angeles. He hadn't even been permitted to be a delegate to the convention. Mr. Kennedy wisely left all of this Texas feudin' and fightin' to Mr. Johnson, as he flew off to St. Louis the following day.

The "Corn Ball Express" which was going to be Mr. Johnson's base of operations for the next few weeks soon started to roll all over the South. Bobby Baker, who was in charge of this "Campaign in Dixie," arranged for the people who would come aboard at each stop, saw that there was plenty of Cutty Sark or brandy, and briefed Mr. Johnson on what had been done in the Congress for each area. "Bobby, turn that Yellow Rose down," Mr. Johnson would shout if the music got a little loud and he wanted to do some talking. This whistle-stop special rambled along through the cotton fields, tobacco farms, peaches and peanuts, to the very heart of darkest Southland.

"What do you hear from Lyndon?" Mr. Kennedy said to me one day. I said, "He's putting on a great show down there in the South. He's on his own and he loves it, at least that is what the reporters are saying when they come into the office after they have been riding with him."

Mr. Johnson received some brickbats in his Dixie Campaign and every now and then there would be signs along the trackside meetings accusing him of betraying the South. The influential editor of a leading Richmond newspaper warned, "If Kennedy advisers imagine the South has any deep affection for Lyndon Johnson they are wholly mistaken. He is widely regarded as a renegade, turncoat and opportunist who plays footsie with the liberals."

But, then, staunch segregationist Senator James Eastland held an hour-long TV interview supporting his friend Lyndon Johnson. Senator Eastland told the Mississippi voters, "Lyndon Johnson took everything relating to integration out of those civil rights bills. He has always opposed Congress' implementation of the segregation decisions of the Supreme Court."

This statement pleased Eastland's followers, but worried northern liberals who continued to feel uneasy about just where Johnson stood. Nevertheless, southern moderates praised Senator Johnson for speaking for the rights and liberties of all Americans and speaking this way in some strong anti-civil rights areas.

Johnson's campaigning according to newspaper reporters varied from town to town and city to city, but it always ended up with a "wheeling-dealing" session with local "court house" politicians in the forward part of the observation car. These politicians usually were not for Mr. Kennedy because he was not an organization man.

The old train would puff and toot into a station, and stop where all of the people had gathered. Naturally, the local committee had arranged for a colorful welcome with flags, placards and a full ration of "hoopin' and hollerin'." The placards would read "Hurray LBJ," "America Needs Kennedy–Johnson," or "Dixie is not for Nixie." Children strutted around with American flags and sprinkled throughout the crowd would appear a number of Confederate flags, and at some stations the band played "Dixie." Then Mr. Johnson would appear at the end of the observation car.

Mr. Johnson talked to these people in language they understood. Here he was in home territory, and he communicated in a way that Mr. Kennedy could not and would not. Johnson pleaded with them to "vote for the party of your fathers." He would tell them about his own life down in the southern part of Texas and somewhere along in his speaking he would remark, "This grandson of a 'federate soldier' feels lahk I'm in may-ty tall cotton, let me tell you." Remarks like that were effective, and produced a show of the stars and bars and a chorus of rebel yells.

Many, many writers have written about his visit to Culpeper, Virginia because it is typical of Johnson's whistle-stops. The train pulled into Culpeper and stopped where the people had gathered, but this crowd was just a little out of the ordinary. At first glance, it seemed another gathering of excited country folk, a whistle-stop. But this crowd had been salted with carloads of employees from the various Texas congressional offices who had driven down from Washington. These Texans had dressed up to look like small-towners and they blended right in with the local people, though their voices and laughter were a shade or two louder. When Mr. Johnson came out the back door and onto the platform he said, "I just want to tell you how happy I am that you would come here and howdy and shake with us this mornin' . . . I'd appreciate so much if you'all'd come just a little bit closer. You make us feel so wonderful to come out here and look us in the eye and give us a chance to—uh—press the flesh with you." When the train started to leave he shouted, "They tell me we cain't carry Virginia. I don't believe it, do you?" When he said this those Texas voices came out with a roar: "No!" Then he made that unforgettable remark, which almost destroyed the Republican candidate: "When they tell you that, you just ask 'em, 'What did Richard Nixon ever do for Culpeper?' " (Incidentally, Culpeper voted for Nixon.)

Mr. Johnson was very much at home in this back platform campaigning. He was colorful and effective. The press coverage was tremendous and he stirred up enthusiasm for the Democratic candidate. But where he was really at home, was working behind the scenes with the men and women who got on and off at each stop, or rode along on the train. It was to them that he argued, "Don't desert the party of your fathers, particularly when it is about to win. Don't throw away your preferred status in Congress. You know as well as I that Southerners only serve as Committee Chairmen when the Democrats are in the White House. And don't antagonize the Democratic men of power who can make or break your district by decisions on federal spending."

I joined the Kennedy campaign caravan in the middle of October, and from that time on I was so busy trying to keep up with the top candidate that I didn't have too much time to think about his "stand in." Of course, Johnson was not only campaigning in the South, he was also going into other parts of the country. In turn, Kennedy also campaigned in the South. In fact, one of his first swings was through Maryland, Tennessee, West Virginia, and North Carolina.

One of the important side benefits of even a grueling campaign is that it gives a Presidential candidate the chance to look over the new crop of politicians who are coming up. He can compare those old political hands he has had to be friendly with because of their established power with those he might wish to associate with when he has gained a position of more independence.

Mr. Kennedy found in North Carolina a part of the

country and a man which seemed particularly attractive and promising to him. The man was Terry Sanford, then running for Governor of North Carolina. Mr. Kennedy had enjoyed meeting him at the convention in Los Angeles in July where Mr. Sanford had declared for Mr. Kennedy. He had withstood the toughest pressure which resulted and he had helped convince some southern delegates that a Kennedy Administration would be exactly what the new forward-looking part of the South needed. Now, he accompanied Mr. Kennedy on his campaign through North Carolina.

In Greenville, North Carolina on September 17, 1960, Mr. Kennedy said "I have discussed the problem of our rural areas with your next Governor—Terry Sanford. I like his approach. We see eye to eye on his 'positive program' for better research, for better roads, for better cooperation between farmer and businessman and Government to bring the processing plants and other light industries into rural areas for balanced growth. I am going to look to Terry Sanford for further advice in working out a sound program for Federal-State cooperation to reverse the disgraceful neglect of our rural population under eight years of Ezra Taft Benson . . ."

Terry Sanford, a former special agent for the Federal Bureau of Investigation in 1941 and 1942, enlisted in the United States Army, where he saw action in five campaigns in Italy, France, Belgium, and Germany. He participated in the invasion of Southern France and the Battle of the Bulge. He returned home and resumed his studies at the University of North Carolina where he was awarded the LL.B. degree in 1946. From 1946 to 1948 he served as assistant director of the Institute of Government at Chapel Hill, seat of the University of North Carolina. In 1948 he started practicing law in Fayetteville and in 1949 he was elected President of the North Carolina Young Democratic Clubs. From 1950 to 1953 he served as a member of the State Ports Authority under appointment by Governor W. Kerr Scott, and in 1953-1954 he was a member of the North Carolina State Senate. A staunch supporter of Scott, Sanford served as state manager for the Governor's successful campaign for the United States Senate in 1954.

In addition to his political activities on a state level, Sanford had taken an active part in national politics. Having previously served as a delegate to the 1956 Democratic National Convention, he played a major role in helping to bring about the nomination of Mr. Kennedy in July 1960. Sanford was the first of the southern leaders attending the convention to leave the camp of Lyndon B. Johnson and join the Kennedy forces. He seconded Kennedy's nomination and thereby won himself not only the support and friendship of the Kennedy Administration but also a role as a key figure in gaining southern support for the Administration's major proposals.

As he traveled to Charlotte, Greensboro, Greenville, and Raleigh, North Carolina, Kennedy spoke in a language slightly different from that of Johnson. He talked about issues, he talked about international affairs, he opened up the world of science and economics to his audience. He described his relationship between federal inactivity and local unemployment. He used his most effective weapon—his rapier wit—to slash at the Republicans and to make his audience listen intently; he quoted poetry to touch their hearts. He did not ask what Nixon had done for Greensboro, but what Khrushchev might do to the United States.

This was the approach native to his mind and temperament. This is how people expected a Presidential candidate to speak. And he was effective, just as Lyndon Johnson was effective, in combining his public plain-folks technique with the hard back room bargaining and tough explaining of the political realities.

Mr. Kennedy's approach in North Carolina was like his national campaigning, and quite a bit different than the way he campaigned in Texas where it seemed necessary to dwell on military production and defense expenditure and to mention Sam Houston and the Alamo as often as possible.

Certainly Mr. Johnson was doing well out in the Middle West. He was biting at the Republicans in his typical campaign style. At one whistle-stop in Kansas, he said that the Kansas farmers should sue Mr. Ezra Benson, Eisenhower's Secretary of Agriculture, for non-support. Mr. Kennedy liked this line and he used it in several of his speeches.

Though the campaign was coming to a close the feudin' and fightin' was still going on in Texas. Those 24 electoral votes were too precious to lose through intra-party squabbling, and there seemed nothing else for Mr. Kennedy to do but to go back to the Lone Star State for another round of appearances if he didn't want the stars to eclipse one another. Off we went to Amarillo where Mr. Kennedy was going to speak at the airport. Mr. Johnson and Lady Bird were waiting for us.

Then I heard Howard Baird, the pilot of the *Caroline*, say, "Mr. Johnson wants to ride with Mr. Kennedy on this plane when we go to Wichita Falls." Mr. Kennedy immediately answered, "That's ridiculous. He has his own plane. It wouldn't be practical for both of us to be traveling together." And then he added, "He will probably get mad. You know how sensitive he is, so kind of soften up what you say to him." I gave the message to one of our advance men and I guess they got the message across because he did not travel with us.

To say that the Amarillo airport was unusual would be an understatement of almost criminal proportion. It seemed as though man and nature had joined forces at Amarillo to make it unbearable for us to do anything. Since there was always so much work to be done on the plane, I usually didn't go out to hear Mr. Kennedy speak. But this time I was curious. We were told that people in Amarillo were so hostile they would have nothing to do with anyone wearing a Kennedy button. It was the local equivalent to wearing a hammer and sickle. I wanted to see for myself what they would do when they met Mr. Kennedy face to face.

When I stepped off the plane I was almost blown into outer space by the strong Texas wind. I finally made it to the section where the people were pushing and shoving trying to get a look at the candidate. The blast of planes taking off and landing was added to the snarl of the wind and the noise was deafening. It seemed as though planes were landing and taking off one a minute. As one of the planes zoomed near to the ground Mr. Kennedy remarked, "That must be Dick coming in." The few who heard his remark laughed and applauded. Then he said, "I understand Vice President Nixon is arriving in Texas with a rescue squad—Nelson Rockefeller, the President of the United States, Henry Cabot Lodge, and now they are adding three new members to the rescue squad, who are advising him on how to win the election—Landon, Hoover and Dewey. We can't lose." Once again those few who heard him over the wind and the planes laughed and applauded.

As one aircraft continued to race its motors, Mr.

Kennedy shouted, "They can't stop the truth anyway. I don't care how much that engine warms up."

Then, suddenly, Mr. Johnson, who was standing in front of Mr. Kennedy, flew into a rage. He scowled, then he frowned. He jerked at his broad-rimmed Texas hat and raised his hand toward the culprit plane with its shrieking engine. He shook a threatening finger and let out a tremendous howl accompanied by some very strong language. Lady Bird, seeing how angry her husband was, added her shouts of protest. Mr. Kennedy looked at Mr. Johnson and then at Lady Bird, and reached forward and laid his hand on his excited running-mate's shoulder in an effort to calm him. If Mr. Kennedy was disturbed, he didn't show it for he went on to say, "This is the busiest airport I have ever been in."

In Wichita Falls, Mr. Kennedy told his audience that in the light of Nixon's savage assaults on the Democrats, including himself and Johnson, it would be difficult for them to work with him in the Senate if he should become President. ". . . in 1960 he called me a liar, in 1960 he called Lyndon an ignoramus. Lyndon said he called me one, too. I said he called him one. He called me rash, inexperienced, reckless and uninformed. But he called Lyndon an ignoramus. Will he sit down and work with him?"

In another part of the state, Congressman Wright Patman of Texarkana was telling the people in his district that they were faced with the very same problem in 1960 as people in 1928. In 1960 Kennedy, the Catholic, is running against Nixon, the Quaker. In 1928 Al Smith, the Catholic, was battling it out against Herbert Hoover, the Quaker. Then he said, "What did the people do? They chose the Quaker and so we quaked for four years. Let's not make the same mistake again."

Throughout the campaign the American people were given the opportunity to see two different approaches to political campaigning in action.

Time was running out. "I don't want to be sitting in Massachusetts on November 8th," Mr. Kennedy was saying, "and have that phone ringing and saying, 'We are doing fine,' and Lyndon call me and say, 'We just lost Texas.' I want him to call me on the phone and say, 'Texas is leading the nation in the Democratic camp.' "

Mr. Kennedy and his wife, Jackie, voted in Boston on November 8th. Mr. Johnson and his wife, Lady Bird, in Johnson City.

"It's Up To You," Mr. Kennedy had said in an article in the *Democratic Digest*, to the American people. "Once again, this election and the Nation's course for the next four years is up to you."

CHAPTER

IX

First Legislative Fight

FOUR YEARS! Four years to get this country moving again.

How about Lyndon Johnson? Was he ready to move? In his very first test—the rump session—he was a failure! During that period he did absolutely nothing to merit the accolades and big build up of his great legislative knowledge. He had even been called by some members of the press as the greatest Majority Leader of all time. The rump session seemed to puncture that balloon. Would he continue to fail?

Just two days after New Year's, 1961, President Kennedy and I were in sunny Palm Beach, Florida, instead of shivering through the January chill back in Washington. We were going over the mail, working on Inauguration details and on the move we would soon make to the White House.

"Mrs. Lincoln, accept these two invitations," said Mr. Kennedy. This was significant. They were for receptions, the first honoring Speaker Sam Rayburn to be held in the East Room of the Mayflower Hotel on January 16th and the other at the home of Philip Graham at 2920 R Street, N.W., on January 19—the night before the Inauguration. These two men, Rayburn and Graham! Never would I forget how desperately they had worked to promote the candidacy of Johnson rather than Kennedy for the Presidency, especially out at the convention in Los Angeles.

It was apparent that Mr. Kennedy was overlooking the rump session and the campaign maneuvers, in his effort to gain friendly relations with Mr. Johnson, Speaker Rayburn, and their supporters.

Mr. Kennedy paused. He had picked up a task force memorandum which had come in the mail that morning. As he sat there thumbing through the pages I recalled that it was here in Palm Beach just six years ago that Mr. Kennedy had been recuperating from a serious back operation, and was looking forward to returning to the United States Senate in March. Earlier he had written a letter to Majority Leader Johnson, applying for a place on one of three Senate committees—Finance, Appropriations, or Foreign Relations. He had received a rather friendly and somewhat encouraging reply from Mr. Johnson. In it Mr. Johnson had said, "It has been many years since I have enjoyed working with anyone as much as I have with you." Then, three days later, Mr. Kennedy received another letter. This time Mr. Johnson said he was sorry, but it was impossible to work out an assignment for Kennedy on any of the committees he had requested.

Mr. Kennedy jogged me back to reality by saying, "Let's get on with the mail," but before we could go on the telephone rang. "Yes," he was saying, "Lyndon is not going to resign his Senate seat until just before January twentieth. Yes, that's right. He will be on hand tomorrow to help direct the organization of the Senate." That meant William A. Blakely, the man slated to take Mr. Johnson's seat in the Senate, would not be sworn in until just before the Inauguration. I had read that Mr. Blakely, once a cowboy, had become extremely wealthy through some oil transaction.

Mr. Johnson had been re-elected to the United States Senate in Texas at the same time that he had been elected Vice President. Therefore, when the Senate convened on January 4th, 1961, he was sworn in with the other Senators.

And then came his second legislative failure. By being sworn in with the other Senators and therefore being present at the Democratic Congress, Mr. Johnson hoped to retain his control over the Senate. He attended the Democratic caucus on January 4th, where Senator Mansfield proposed that Mr. Johnson, as Vice President, be given the right to preside over future Democratic caucuses. That proposal backfired. Even Senators with whom he had wheeled and dealed protested, and the proposal boomeranged. However, Johnson was able to retain his image, because Mike Mansfield, the newly elected Majority Leader, a very unassuming man, said that he would be satisfied with a small office. Therefore, Mr. Johnson kept his plush office near the Senate floor, and Bobby Baker retained his job as Secretary to the Senate.

Once again Mr. Kennedy was disappointed at Johnson's failure to achieve his objective with the Senate. However, he, of course, continued to work with him, cooperating in making appointments that Mr. Johnson requested and authorizing the office staff that he wanted. Kennedy was anxious to give his Vice President authority and a place in the New Frontier and not to relegate him to the meaningless place of many former Vice Presidents.

As evidence of this intention, when Mr. Johnson wanted to know if Bill Daniel, the son of Governor Price Daniel of Texas, had been cleared for an appointment as Governor of Guam, Mr. Kennedy said he would check on it personally. It was natural for Mr. Johnson to be interested in having this appointment go through because Price Daniel, together with Speaker Sam Rayburn, was the man who had set up the "Johnson for President" headquarters down there in Austin.

Then he asked Mr. Kennedy to have someone on

his staff work with his Administrative Assistant, Walter Jenkins, in placing many of his staff members. He no doubt had to do some pruning because as the Senator from Texas he received more each year for office hire than he would as Vice President. And, through the patronage system in the Senate, as the Majority Leader, Mr. Johnson had about 100 appointees scattered through Senate committees and the various Senate payrolls.

But the biggest request of all was that *all* job appointments for Texans, in or out of the state, were to be cleared by him. When he made this request I typed out a memo to be sent to Mr. Kennedy's brother Bob, his Appointment Secretary, Kenny O'Donnell, and his Legislative Assistant, Larry O'Brien. Mr. Kennedy signed it.

Every time I turned around a new Texan was being considered for an appointment. One of the first was John B. Connally, Johnson's "right arm" throughout his campaign for the Presidency. He was proposed for the office of Secretary of the Navy and he accepted long before the Inauguration.

Repeatedly, it seemed to me that Mr. Johnson was more interested in personal patronage power and his own image-making than in the success of Kennedy's legislative battles.

Still, I was living through many of the most exciting days of my life and waiting for the Inauguration. Mr. Johnson and his whereabouts were forgotten in my concentration on the man in the world spotlight —Mr. Kennedy.

Mr. Kennedy started the rounds of Inaugural festivities by going to the reception for Speaker Sam Rayburn at the Mayflower Hotel. Then, a couple of nights later, he went to a reception and buffet honoring Mr. Johnson and Lady Bird at the Statler Hilton. Mr. Kennedy stayed at this reception for about thirty minutes, mixing and mingling with the guests. And, despite the snow, he and Mrs. Kennedy went to the reception at Philip Graham's home the night before the Inauguration.

The Inauguration, which fell on a Friday, was, of course, a day I will never forget. However, it made no difference to Mr. Kennedy, now President, that the next day was Saturday. He was eager and anxious to get his Administration moving. (And I shared his feeling.) In fact, I was too excited to feel exhausted from all of the festivities the day and night before. So we all went to work in our new offices in the West Wing the following morning.

I was in my office at 9:00 A.M. and I barely had time to put my feet under my desk or get my coat off when Mr. Kennedy burst in, asking about the mail. Also, he wanted to be sure to see Speaker Rayburn and Mr. Johnson the first thing the following Monday morning. Then he added, "I want to meet with the legislative leaders at 9:00 A.M. on Tuesday morning. Take down these names—Rayburn, McCormack, Al-bert, Mansfield, Humphrey, Smathers, and Johnson. Give these names to Larry and tell him to tell these men that I would like to see them on Tuesday."

He was going into action and wanted to get his congressional team working on his legislative program right away. To mix a metaphor, there was one sly old fox in the ointment: Chairman Howard W. Smith with his stranglehold over the House Rules Committee and, thus, over all legislation. Smith's great, almost fantastic power, exercised on behalf of the conservative bloc, had long galled liberals.

The Kennedy liberals appealed to Speaker Sam Rayburn. Could he do something to break Smith's grip? They suggested purging Congressman William Colmer of Mississippi, and thus depriving Smith of a southern vote. Colmer was even more conservative than Smith. He had supported the independent Presidential-elector slate in Mississippi, not the Kennedy–Johnson ticket. Speaker Rayburn hesitated since he thought that action against Colmer might hurt the leadership's relations in the South. Instead, he came up with a compromise plan to enlarge the House Rules Committee from 12 to 15. By this action, the Democrats would have 10 members, and the Republicans 5 instead of the existing 8 and 4. As it now stood, a combination of two southern Democrats and four Republicans, by a 6-6 tie vote, could block any legislation it thought was too liberal—and to this coalition, almost all positive legislation was liberal.

Speaker Rayburn assured Mr. Kennedy that there would be no difficulty in getting this compromise proposal passed. The President was gratified because in nearly half a century of service in the House, Mr. Rayburn had rarely known defeat on an issue that was important to him. Still Mr. Kennedy wasn't taking any chances. In spite of this assurance, he wanted to talk to Mr. Rayburn, Mr. Johnson, and the legislative leaders before the House voted on the resolution the following Thursday.

Monday morning came. At 8:35 Mr. Kennedy asked me to get Mr. Johnson on the phone. They discussed the meeting with the legislative leaders. Then, Johnson, always mindful of his image, had a suggestion. He would come to the Mansion about a half an hour before the meeting would take place so that they could talk matters over and then walk together to the West Wing to the 9:00 meeting. Mr. Kennedy agreed, and I put it on his Tuesday schedule.

It was a busy day with discussions with the various Presidential advisors. Mr. Kennedy was also working on his State of the Union speech to be given the following Monday. In the midst of all of this turmoil came the news from Capitol Hill that the Republican caucus had voted overwhelmingly to oppose the resolution enlarging the Rules Committee. Mr. Kennedy dropped what he was doing. He started marshaling his forces. "Get Congressman Frank Thompson of New Jersey on the telephone," he said to me. After he had talked to Democratic Congressman Thompson he asked me to call Congressman Richard Bolling of Missouri. He wanted these two young Congressmen to start getting votes for the resolution. "I can't lose this one," he said. "I just can't go down the drain in my very first try."

There was a continual buzzing of voices as the legislative leaders filed into the Cabinet Room for their 9:00 o'clock meeting with Mr. Kennedy. They milled around my office, and while they were waiting, several called their offices. "I'm down at the White House," they would proudly say. A little before 9:00 out came Mr. Kennedy and Mr. Johnson. As they walked down the colonnade toward the Cabinet Room, Mr. Johnson was talking and gesturing. As they reached the door of the Cabinet Room, Mr. Kennedy motioned for Mr. Johnson to enter while he continued on to his office.

Mr. Kennedy stopped by his desk, glanced at his schedule for the day, had a few words with his Appointment Secretary, Kenny O'Donnell, looked at the clock, pushed back the hair from his forehead, seemed to wait a moment, then slowly walked through the door to my office. He smiled and nodded as he passed my desk and then opened the door to the Cabinet Room where the legislative leaders were standing awaiting his arrival.

For about an hour they discussed procedures, the economic outlook, revenue, the State of the Union speech, the legislative program, but most of all the pressing Rules Committee vote. The minutes of all these meetings came across my desk.

The meeting broke up. Mr. Johnson followed Mr. Kennedy right into the President's office. Before the door closed I overheard Mr. Kennedy say, "I guess the Senate confirmed John Connally as Secretary of the Navy yesterday." "Yeah," Johnson remarked. "John's a good boy."

The scene that I saw as I went in and out of the office with telephone messages during the next fifteen minutes was one that I was going to see many, many, many times whenever Johnson was in that office alone with Mr. Kennedy. Kennedy was sitting at his desk fiddling with papers. In front of the desk stood Johnson, slightly bent to the right. His right arm was raised and he was pointing his finger. In a loud voice he would preface his remarks with, "Now let me tell you, Jack." And, at the end of each sentence, he jabbed his finger toward Mr. Kennedy. The President said very little, but continued to shuffle through the papers on his desk. The gist of the whole conversation seemed to be how Johnson was going to get the votes needed to pass the Rules Committee resolution. Finally, Mr. Kennedy stood up from his chair, brushed aside his hair, looked at his schedule and said, "That's fine, Lyndon." Johnson turned and ambled out of the room.

By Wednesday, Congressmen Thompson and Bolling, who had been working very hard on getting the needed votes for the Rules Committee resolution, felt uneasy. They thought Mr. Rayburn's head-count was too close for comfort. They reported this to Mr. Kennedy who, in turn, got in touch with the leadership. The leadership then went into a huddle and came up with the idea of postponing the showdown vote to give the Administration more time to work on the members to make sure that they had the necessary votes. They postponed the vote on the proposal until the following Tuesday.

I couldn't help thinking that wherever Mr. Kennedy turned road blocks always appeared. Although he tried to assume a "hands off" approach, at his very first press conference there was no doubt in anyone's mind what he wanted. He wanted the Rayburn proposal to increase the membership of the Rules Committee adopted. His own prestige was at stake.

He had one more *forum* before the vote. His State of the Union message was scheduled to be delivered before the joint session of Congress on Monday. At 8:45 Monday morning he received a call from Mr. Johnson who wanted to see him before he went to the Hill as he had something to tell him concerning the Rules Committee proposal. When Johnson arrived he told Mr. Kennedy that he thought that the Rules Committee proposal would be defeated.

After all the confidence that he had previously expressed, his statement was like a slap in the face to

Mr. Kennedy. Mr. Kennedy didn't waste a minute before whipping into action. First he called his brother Bob and between them they decided to take over. The outcome was too important to permit the President to rely solely on Rayburn and Johnson. He then told Johnson that he would like to meet with him, Speaker Rayburn, Bob, Larry O'Brien and Kenny O'Donnell at about 3:00 following his State of the Union message and the Capitol luncheon. By 3:05 P.M. all of these men were gathered together and working hard. It was the first time all of these men had ever worked together so closely.

At noon on the day of the "big" vote the galleries were filled to capacity. The House convened. The Chaplain gave his usual prayer. There was a tenseness and a feeling of great anxiety as Speaker Sam Rayburn pounded his gavel. In his deep voice, he announced that the legislation to be considered was the Rules Committee proposal. Some Congressmen made speeches. They were only interested in the voting. And, about that, there was no secret. It was going to be close. In fact, Mr. Rayburn's head-count said that the Kennedy forces would win by a vote of 217 to 212.

The Clerk started to call the roll. As he came to the very last name on the list it turned out that 64 Democrats, all from the South and border states voted *against* the resolution, while 22 Republicans, most from the urban Northeast, crossed over the party line to vote to expand the committee.

The final vote was exactly what had been predicted —217 for the proposal, 212 against. As soon as the voting was over, Larry O'Brien called—and told me the news! He asked me to give the vote to President Kennedy. Although he had someone in his office at the time, I rushed in with the message. Mr. Kennedy took the card I handed him, read the message, smiled slightly and went on talking to his visitor. But I knew that he was extremely pleased.

A little later on, as Mr. Kennedy was sitting in his office talking to Ted Sorensen, Speaker Rayburn called. Mr. Kennedy turned to Mr. Sorensen and said, "Oh, the Speaker is calling me. Just a minute." He picked up the receiver and as I walked back toward my office I overheard him say, "Yes, I am glad we won, too. Many thanks for all of your efforts."

I went back to my typing. It was getting late and I knew it wouldn't be long before Mr. Kennedy would leave for the Mansion. As he so often did, he walked into my office, stopped at the corner of my desk and thumbed through the letters and papers I had put in a box marked for his attention—letters for him to sign or pictures to autograph.

As he walked toward the door to leave, he turned to me and said, "By the way, did Mr. Johnson call me?" When I said to him, "No, he didn't, Mr. President," he paused for a second, with a quizzical expression on his face. Then he turned and walked out.

CHAPTER

X

Mr. Johnson at the White House

IT SEEMED as if Mr. Johnson would have failed on this Rules Committee legislation if he had been left to himself. I knew that Mr. Kennedy was very disappointed, that he had expected a lot more and had been led to expect more. He now realized that his main source of strength was himself, and that he would have to look elsewhere for help on legislation. Yet the Administration was only two weeks old!

Mr. Johnson, on the other hand, started out, from the very beginning, to spend as much time as he possibly could around the White House. There were two doors in my office that opened out on the colonnade that led to the South Lawn. Mr. Johnson chose to enter the West Wing through one of the doors of my office. Nearly every morning he would open that door, grunt and pause for a moment to look around to see what was going on. He would look into the President's office to see if Mr. Kennedy was there, or pause to talk to people who came in and out of my office. If there was nothing to attract his attention, he would amble over to the other door and go out into the hall.

Many a morning he stood before my desk and discussed with staff members how Senators and Congressmen stood on various issues. Frequently I thought his references were commonplace. One time he compared a certain Senator to a steer. When the listener said, "Why do you call him a steer?" Mr. Johnson replied, "That's a bull who's lost his social standing."

One morning he was a little late coming through the door and when he arrived Mr. Kennedy was standing near my desk. They exchanged greetings and Mr. Johnson proceeded on his way to the hall. After Mr. Johnson had gone, Mr. Kennedy turned to me and said, "Does he use this door very often?" "Every day," I replied. "What is he doing in these offices?" Mr. Kennedy asked.

I checked and learned that Mr. Johnson's driver let him out near the sidewalk leading to the President's office on the South Lawn. He would then walk up that sidewalk past the President's office to the door of my office. From my office he went out into the hall which led to the reception room. It was in this room that the newspaper men gathered. It was only a short distance from that room to his office in the Executive Office Building across the street.

By coming into my office, Mr. Johnson was creating the image of working closely with Mr. Kennedy at all times, especially if he was in the outer office when any of the Cabinet men or other officials came in. Also, when he came out into the reception room from the area of the President's office the press would obviously get the same impression.

Another major concern of Mr. Johnson was the invitation lists. On these he would call me and say, "Mrs. Lincoln, I've just looked over some of the lists of dinners to be given by Mr. Kennedy and on one of them I do not find my name. I wonder if you would check and see if there has been a mistake." I told him that I would certainly look into it. When I did, I learned that it was a dinner of personal friends. No one could understand why Mr. Johnson had asked to be invited. When I told the President about Mr. Johnson's call, he said, "You mean he called and wanted to be invited?" I told him that was correct and he said, "What did you tell him?" "I told him I would look into it." Then Mr. Kennedy said, "Call him and tell him that you have checked and you found that there was no mistake."

Another time the Vice President called and said, "Mrs. Lincoln, be a good girl and see that I get invited to all the meetings in the White House." I didn't mention this call to Mr. Kennedy because I felt he had more important things to think about than making sure that Mr. Johnson was invited to all the meetings. Further, I was sure that if he wanted Mr. Johnson at a meeting, he would make sure that he was invited.

Mr. Johnson once told the reporter Mary McGrory, "The other day he [Mr. Kennedy] asked me to go to the congressional reception at the White House even though he hadn't invited me."

I chuckled right out loud when I came to the part, "though he hadn't invited me." Now he was trying to create the image that Mr. Kennedy didn't want him around, although the truth is that since this particular party was for Members of the House of Representatives, the House leadership was given the honor of "co-hosting" the reception. Mr. Johnson would have a similar function at parties for the Senate.

I put this article, together with other items and mail in Mr. Kennedy's box on the corner of my desk. As Mr. Kennedy stopped by on his way to the Mansion, he saw this article and, with a twinkle in his eye, said, "I've read it." It happened that in the box there was also a card upon which I had written, "Do you want to invite the Vice President to the luncheon on Friday?" Mr. Kennedy hesitated and then, as he started to walk out of the door, he turned around and said, "The answer to that question is 'No.' "

The twenty Johnson staff members had been taken care of, but I never found out whether they stayed in the office in the Capitol or whether they were scattered around in Mr. Johnson's various offices. He had offices up at the Capitol near the Senate floor and offices in the Senate Office Building. He also wanted one in or near the West Wing of the White House. He had suggested having an office next to Mr. Kennedy's but when the President heard this he was flabbergasted. "I have never heard of such a thing," he said. "Give him an office over in the Executive Office Building right across the street."

Apparently Mr. Johnson also wanted an office in one of the government departments. I got a call from the Department of Health, Education and Welfare one day asking me if I knew anything about the office that Mr. Johnson was going to have down there. When I asked Mr. Kennedy if he knew anything about it, he said "No" and that was the last I heard of it.

There was also a time when he was checking on homes around Lafayette Square, the park that is directly north of the White House. There were no homes available, and, in any case, there was some thought of removing some of those houses to make way for federal buildings. Some people collect stamps or butterflies or match covers. It seemed that Mr. Johnson collected offices—and probably had more of them than any other government official before or since.

Mr. Kennedy and Mr. Johnson had different views concerning the giving and receiving of gifts. Kennedy never showered gifts on people nor did he ever accept them, whether he was in the Senate or the White House. When we first moved into the White House, he laid down the rule that only gifts valued at $15.00 or less could be accepted. From the first day, we returned all of the expensive gifts.

Gifts to Mr. Johnson were different. He was accustomed to showering gifts on people and accepting them, regardless of value. And he wanted recipients not to just be glad to receive them, but really excited about them. The more excited and happy they were, the happier he was.

Since he had this attitude, it was natural for Mr. Johnson to tell Mr. Kennedy one day as they were walking to the oval office after a legislative leaders' breakfast, that he was having some cattle sent to the Kennedy home in Middleburg, Virginia. He also added that he was sending along a horse by the name of Tex for Caroline. Then he went on to say that he would like to be on hand when they arrived in Middleburg so that he could see that they were in good order. Most of all, however, he wanted to see how the Kennedys reacted when they saw them.

Accepting these gifts was very embarrassing to Mr. Kennedy because of the code of ethics he was setting up for government employees. However, he sensed that Mr. Johnson would be very disturbed if he did otherwise. He invited him to come to Middleburg shortly after the cattle and horse arrived. Mr. Kennedy had a problem, however. He didn't know where he was going to keep them.

One morning I looked out on the South Lawn and I noticed a new pony eating the grass. Is that Tex? I thought. When I mentioned it to Mr. Kennedy he said, "Oh, that's right, we promised Mr. Johnson that we would have our picture taken with him and this horse. Find out if Mrs. Kennedy is available and if she is, when Caroline comes out with her nursery school maybe we could get a picture of all of us, Mr. Johnson and that animal." I checked. Mrs. Kennedy would be available. Since Mr. Johnson would be attending a meeting in the Cabinet Room, he too would be available. It was all arranged.

Mr. and Mrs. Kennedy stood on one side of Tex and on the other side stood Mr. Johnson holding the reins, while in the saddle on the back of the horse sat Caroline. You could tell Mr. Johnson was really enjoying this, because he strolled around patting Caroline on the head and slapping the horse . . .

Shortly after this "family portrait" session, Mr. Johnson came through my office and spied Caroline sitting by my desk drawing pictures. His face lit up with a smile, which ironed out some of the furrows and lines. "Do you know who I am, Caroline?" he said. Caroline looked at him, then looked at me. She really didn't know so she didn't say anything. I said to her, "That's Mr. Johnson, Caroline." And then he said, "That's right. I'm your Uncle Lyndon, remember? I'm the one who gave you that fine riding horse, Tex." Caroline, who was very shy, simply muttered, "Oh." Then he went on, "Now remember what I told you, Caroline, I want you to call me 'Uncle Lyndon' whenever you see me. Will you remember to do that?"

Then he bent over, patted her on the head, and walked out of the room.

After he had gone, Caroline looked at me and said, "Is he really my uncle?" "Well, if he is," I said to her, "he would have to be your daddy's brother, or maybe your mommy's brother." Caroline giggled and said, "Oh, Mrs. Lincoln."

Johnson must have realized that he had failed to make any headway with Caroline, because many, many other times when he passed through she was in my office. She never ran up to him and called him "Uncle Lyndon," nor did he ever mention it to her again.

At this time he was anxious to create a new image for himself. He was giving out interviews saying that he was "real" happy with his new role as the understudy to the President. He also said that he was no longer the flamboyant leader he used to be; he had become more scholarly and was reading all the books he could find that could help him meet his new responsibilities.

He was also saying that his relationship with Mr. Kennedy was excellent. Then the following statement was issued, which fit my reasoning about why he came through my office every day. He reported that it was his custom to see Mr. Kennedy many, many times during the day.

An article that appeared in the New York *Post* written by Mary McGrory said, "He has, according to his associates, after a rather lonely and wistful interlude, accepted his new status as presiding officer of the Senate instead of its master.

"Not even those who opposed his selection as presiding officer of the Senate party caucuses have found fault with his performance. They say he has been unobtrusive and helpful. The leadership still consults him."

Then she also revealed what Mr. Kennedy had known for a long time. She said, "During the long hours when the Administration's unemployment bill was being passed through a series of tight votes, he was in constant attendance in case of a tie but never laid a persuading hand on any sleeve." He himself seemed by his actions to be admitting that he had a less important role in the Senate leadership.

It was precisely for this reason that the President was turning to the powerful Senator from Oklahoma, Robert S. Kerr. The new relationship between Senator Kerr and the Kennedy Administration was reflected in a rather whimsical news release put out by Senator Kerr's office in April. It said: "The flowers that bloom in the spring, tra la, have nothing to do with the case, a song goes, but the bright bursts of the red bud and the flowering forsythia lend timely symbolism to new trends in my favorite program—Land, Wood and Water.

"The new climate in the Executive Branch definitely has something to do with the blossoming hopes for great advancements in the development of Oklahoma's natural resources . . .

"President Kennedy himself has put more sunshine into our scene. He requested an additional $4,675,000 for the Arkansas River development program, bringing the total Corps of Engineers budget recommendation for the coming year to $89 million for Oklahoma and related projects . . ."

Mr. Kennedy deeply appreciated the help he was getting from Senator Kerr. To show his appreciation he flew to Oklahoma to participate in the ribbon cutting ceremony that marked the opening of the Ouachita National Forest Road. While he was there he stayed over night at the Kerr Ranch House "Ker-Mac." Senator Kerr was an enormously powerful Senator with a point of view far different from that of Mr. Kennedy. He had even led the fight against the medicare bill so important to the Administration's program. Yet, he helped Mr. Kennedy in many ways and was considered an important ally.

Then, Senator Kerr died. Mr. Kennedy was on his way to Miami from Palm Beach on New Year's Day, 1963, when he learned the news. I was sitting in my hotel room watching the Orange Bowl game on the TV and trying to spot Mr. Kennedy everytime they turned the camera his way. The telephone rang and it was Mr. Johnson who said, "Will you tell Mr. Kennedy that I think I should come to Palm Beach and ride with him on Air Force One to Senator Kerr's funeral." That would give the appearance that they were working closely together and that they had spent the holidays together. He was again thinking about his image.

Again we faced that constant argument with Mr. Johnson about riding on Air Force One with Mr. Kennedy. It cropped up every time the two men were going to make a joint appearance. Time and time again I would hear Mr. Kennedy say, "You don't mean to say that Mr. Johnson is again insisting on riding with me on Air Force One. How many times must I tell him that the President and the Vice President, as a matter of security, should never ride on the same plane?" It seemed that that one thing bothered the Vice President more than anything else.

I knew what the answer would be when I told the President about Mr. Johnson's call. He merely shook his head and said, "Tell him I'll meet him at the Tinker Air Force Base in Oklahoma City." Then in order to soothe what he anticipated would be ruffled feelings, Mr. Kennedy invited him to come to Palm Beach following the funeral. They did not fly back on the same plane.

After Senator Kerr's death, Mike Mansfield played a more active role in pushing legislation in the Senate. Even though Mr. Johnson did very little on legislation, he was regularly invited to attend the Tuesday morning legislative leaders' breakfast—the one that Mr. Kennedy had set up almost the first day he took office. Mr. Kennedy felt that through the efforts of his staff members and leaders like Senator Kerr, he had ended the legislative stalemate that prevailed during much of the Eisenhower Administration. Bills which had been vetoed, or which had failed to pass due to a threat of a veto or lack of Presidential leadership, finally passed. These bills included the minimum wage increase, area redevelopment, housing, water pollution, and long-term foreign aid.

Mr. Johnson also attended many other meetings that were held during the week. Once he complained that he had very little to say at those meetings, but whenever I walked into a meeting, he seemed to be doing all of the talking. There were also comments in the papers that his associates were saying that he participated a great deal at these meetings. He would bring up sticky subjects, they said, and he never let a subject be dropped. For a man who had little to say, that was saying quite a bit.

Among the meetings Mr. Johnson attended were the Cabinet and the National Security Council meetings. In describing these meetings, he once said, "When we go to a meeting, the President sits at the center of the table, I sit to his left. [Yet, the Vice President's place at that table is directly across from the President.] He asks questions, penetrating questions, to bleed everyone for everything they know. He goes around the table and then he asks me, 'What do you think? Can you contribute anything.' Then he and I and the Secretary of Defense or State go into his office for another thirty or forty minutes and maybe just listen to his ideas."

I remember a remark dropped by Mr. Kennedy after one of those meetings, "We never got a thing done today. Lyndon never stopped talking."

During Mr. Kennedy's first year as President, Mr. Johnson had many conferences with him alone. These conferences usually followed the legislative leaders' breakfast when all of the men had walked back to the office from the Mansion. As the leaders filed out of the office and into the hall to go to their offices, Mr. Johnson would hang back. As soon as they were out of earshot he would start his conversation with the usual, "And let me tell you, Jack." Ordinarily, the little chats between Mr. Kennedy and Mr. Johnson did not last very long because of Mr. Kennedy's heavy schedule. There was always someone waiting to see him. According to my records, in the first year these private conferences added up to ten hours and nineteen minutes—by the third year they had fallen off to one hour and fifty-three minutes.

CHAPTER

XI

The Vice President at Work

As I sat in my office in the White House on that unforgettable January day and listened to the newly sworn President give his State of the Union message, I looked at Mr. Johnson and Speaker Rayburn sitting on the rostrum behind him and wondered what was going through their minds. They were not ordinary men. They were leaders who had come a long way to get where they were. I couldn't help thinking that it was going to be difficult for Mr. Johnson suddenly to do everything the "Kennedy way." There were going to be times, I was sure, that his tactics, his views and reactions to problems, would be far different than those of Mr. Kennedy. And, as I had learned during the rump session, he could talk. Therefore, it would be natural for him to argue and try to persuade Mr. Kennedy to proceed his way. I knew Mr.

Kennedy would welcome and value Mr. Johnson's views because of his long legislative experience. Mr. Kennedy would also be mindful of the knowledge Johnson had gained in working for so long with so many members of Congress.

One of the things going through the minds of these two men might have been the President's request that they meet with him at the White House immediately after the luncheon following his address.

What they may not yet have known is the one thing you learned if you were part of the Kennedy team: he expected you to work hard, be on the job, be loyal, and most of all, *get the job done*. He not only wanted you to get it done, but he also wanted it to be done right and in the shortest time possible. This rule applied to Lyndon Johnson and Sam Rayburn, as well as to everyone on the Kennedy team, executive and legislative.

After the episode of the first legislative fight on the Rules Committee, it seemed to me that Mr. Kennedy had a feeling that Mr. Johnson was not as anxious to work with Congress as had been anticipated. So, more and more, Mr. Kennedy relied upon his red-headed, hard-working Special Assistant, the Massachusetts Irishman, Larry O'Brien, to contact the Congressmen, to be "the Man on the Hill." Larry has a mind like a computer, and an almost instinctive understanding of what makes people—and particularly Congress—tick. He was aided by liaison men in every department, who sent him weekly reports on problems, progress, and politics. (Mr. Johnson, Speaker Rayburn, and legislative leaders received copies of this report too.)

These reports were all summarized and included in a legislative progress report. Claude Desautels, Larry's French-speaking assistant, would be pressing constantly. "Mrs. Lincoln, when is the envelope going over to the Mansion tonight?" There was always a mad rush to get it there on time. The envelope he was asking about was Mr. Kennedy's after-dinner reading. He looked forward to reading Larry's report on Monday night before his Tuesday morning breakfast meeting with the legislative leaders in the Mansion.

Mr. Kennedy was deeply concerned about his relations with Congress and frequently attended to the details of maintaining good relations with them himself. "Get Pierre in here," Mr. Kennedy once said to me. Now what's happened? I thought. I got Pierre on the phone. "Mr. Kennedy wants to see you."

"What's this I hear about the White House slamming the door on a special tour for some constituent of Republican Congressman Robert R. Barry of New York?" Mr. Kennedy asked Pierre. "Check on it," he added, "and make sure that you get the word to the press that we are not slamming the door on anyone no matter what party he is in." With this Pierre stalked back through my office leaving a thunderhead of cigar smoke.

The President sent all Congressmen and Senators hand-delivered birthday letters; invited groups of from fifty to sixty to the East Room of the White House for coffee parties; and held bipartisan briefing meetings when major issues were being discussed. Mr. Johnson was included in these coffee parties and in these meetings, but all of the contacts and all of the arrangements were made from offices in the West Wing of the White House.

Now that he had his own legislative machinery rolling and because of Mr. Johnson's seeming reluctance to battle for legislation, Mr. Kennedy decided to use Mr. Johnson's talents in other ways. One was to send him on missions to other countries.

The first mission arose in the early part of March 1961, during a discussion between Mr. Kennedy and McGeorge Bundy, his able and efficient Special Assistant on National Security. As they stood in front of my desk discussing various problems, the question of Senegal came up. Mr. Kennedy was very anxious to have someone from the United States go to Senegal, one of the new African countries, to attend their independence celebration and to extend to them our hand of friendship. He asked Bundy, "How about sending Lyndon?" "Do you want me to check it out with him?" said Mr. Bundy. "Yes, I wish you would feel him out. You know how he is—sort of sensitive. He doesn't like to be pushed into anything."

Mr. Bundy checked it out and Mr. Johnson said he

would be glad to make this trip. A few days later when Mr. Kennedy was talking to Mr. Johnson he said to him, "How about taking Lady Bird with you? Congressman Rooney will no doubt be in touch with you, too."

Now that Mr. Johnson had agreed to make the trip, Mr. Kennedy and Mr. Bundy had another discussion about it. They thought it might also be a good idea for him to make a couple of stops and the President suggested Paris and Geneva. Mr. Bundy checked that out with the State Department which agreed that these stops would be fine.

When the State Department clearance was received, Mr. Kennedy told me to call Mr. Bundy and point out that "since I am going to Paris in May, I wonder if it is a good idea for Johnson to go to Paris. If it is possible for him to go to Rome without going to see the Pope, perhaps that would be a better trip. If not, France would be all right. It would be best if he would key his visit to seeing Gavin and Norstadt at SHAPE and not plan to see de Gaulle."

Mr. Bundy, however, told me that he was sure Congressman Rooney would insist on having an audience with the Pope if they went to Rome. "Okay," said Mr. Kennedy, "call Mr. Bundy and tell him to draft a letter to be sent to Lyndon suggesting the visits to Geneva and Paris."

Mr. Johnson, Lady Bird, Congressman Rooney, and others set off for Dakar and the independence celebration. Lady Bird busied herself with inspecting copper buckets of peanuts while Mr. Johnson had rounds of conferences with the officials of Dakar. While there, the party also went through the local markets and a trade fair. After Geneva, they stopped at Paris where the Vice President conferred with Ambassador Gavin, General Norstadt, and visited the USIA offices.

Mr. Kennedy was very pleased to have Mr. Johnson's report on his talks in Geneva and Paris. I heard him tell Mr. Bundy, "They will be very helpful to me when I visit Europe in May."

Then Mr. Kennedy asked the Vice President to make another trip, this time to Southeast Asia, India, and Pakistan. The relationship between the Soviet Union and the United States had continued to deteriorate and by now was strained almost to the breaking point. Therefore, President Kennedy felt that someone should meet with the officials in these Asian countries to reassure them of our support. According to what the President told me, Mr. Johnson flatly refused. The Vice President recalled how Mr. Eisenhower had sent Mr. Nixon out of the country with sometimes disastrous results, and he didn't think it was an effective plan. He did not want to become a roving ambassador. Mr. Kennedy, his Irish temper rising a bit, stood his ground. After Mr. Johnson had left the office, Mr. Kennedy said, "What do you know about that? Lyndon stalked out of here, mad as a hornet, when I asked him to go to Southeast Asia."

Later on in the day, Mr. Johnson came back for another meeting at the White House. He lumbered through the door of my office, his attitude completely changed. He was all milk and honey. He smiled, patted people on the back, and even took a piece of candy from my candy dish. He went into the Cabinet Room for the meeting as though nothing had happened.

After the meeting he walked with Mr. Kennedy into the President's office. He said he had thought it all over and that it would be a good idea for him to go to Southeast Asia.

We began to make plans. Mr. Kennedy felt that there would be a personal touch added if he also sent his sister Jean Smith and her husband Steve on the trip. Steve, at this time, was with the State Department, so this would be a natural. However, when Mr. Johnson learned that the Smiths might go along, he blew up and remarked that he didn't need a nursemaid traveling with him. My father-in-law, who worked in the reception room, at the Capitol, heard Mr. Johnson telling people that Mr. Kennedy didn't want his Vice President to get too much publicity on his own and, therefore, was sending his sister along.

Nevertheless, Mr. Johnson, Lady Bird, together with Steve and Jean Smith, Carl T. Rowan, Deputy Assistant Secretary of State of Public Affairs, and staff members, finally took off on the 9th of May.

Immediately, reports started coming out of the countries they were visiting. Mr. Johnson, in his own

Texas style of campaigning, was right in his element. He was jumping in and out of his car in the motorcade, kissing babies, slapping men on the back and putting his arms around the women. The Secret Service just couldn't keep up with him. He had thrown the protocol book right out of the window. Of course, we Americans are proud of our informal friendliness with people in other lands, but it might also be said that Mr. Johnson was not completely mindful of the fact that in some countries it was offensive, for example, to kiss people.

We received reports that the Vice President would storm into his hotel room, look around and decide very often that he didn't like it. He barked orders and reprimands like automatic rifle fire and hotel employees would become confused. Yet, after seeing and hearing him shout at people around the Capitol during the rump session, none of these reports seemed far-fetched.

In the two weeks that they were gone, the Vice-Presidential party visited Viet Nam, Laos, Thailand, Taiwan, India, Pakistan, Formosa, and the Philippines. The schedule was staggering and tiring. They attended meetings, dinners, and all kinds of official functions before they returned home.

In Thailand he talked enthusiastically of how the Mekong River which runs through Thailand and South Vietnam could be made into another TVA. He had helped bring public power to the Pedernales down on the LBJ Ranch, he said, and he could see the same thing happening in Southeast Asia. Even though many along the way believed the situation much more complicated even than Texas politics, Mr. Johnson never tired telling Asian leaders, including Nehru, about the details of the Pedernales electric cooperative.

When their plane landed at Andrews Air Force Base on May 24th, Mr. Kennedy had left word at the base for Mr. Johnson and Lady Bird to come to the South Lawn. He wanted to welcome them back personally.

Mr. Kennedy had also asked Cabinet members and other officials to be with him when the flying Johnsons returned. Lady Bird, in a very colorful pink dress, was the first one out of the chopper. She was followed by Mr. Johnson. After a few words from both of them over the microphone Lady Bird left to go home. Mr. Johnson and others went into Mr. Kennedy's office to hear what the Vice President had to say about the trip.

He was exuberant and said Mr. Kennedy was absolutely correct about the timing of this trip. Naturally, that pleased Mr. Kennedy, and he was also delighted to learn that Mr. Johnson's report was just about finished.

As soon as the report arrived I showed it to Mr. Kennedy. "Good," he said. "Will you see that it gets in with my weekend reading?" I skimmed through the pages, but did not see anything about Bashir Ahmad, the camel driver we had been told Mr. Johnson met in Pakistan. Later, I saw Steve Smith and asked him if Mr. Johnson had really invited the camel driver from

Pakistan to visit him. "Oh, he definitely did," Steve replied.

Then came the news. Bashir Ahmad, the camel driver from Pakistan, indeed was coming to visit Mr. Johnson. The Vice President was very displeased with the funny cartoons and articles that were appearing in the papers concerning this visit, and he shouted to the press: "I've been in Southeast Asia and what we need on our side are the camel drivers of the world. The whole world will be watching this reception and listening to what is said about Bashir. He is my guest, and I think it would be cruel and foolish for us to poke fun at him in print."

Mr. Johnson was determined to conduct this visit on a high level, and no visiting dignitary could have received more important treatment. Mr. Johnson not only flew to New York to meet his guest at Idlewild Airport but when he was told that the plane was four hours late, canceled a speech he was scheduled to make in San Antonio that day. He had planned to speak for Henry Gonzalez, who was running for Congress. Mr. Gonzalez was a Texan of Mexican descent, and knowing how resentful many Mexicans feel toward Texans, and the effect it might have on the voters, canceling this appearance must have been a difficult decision to make.

Bashir Ahmad arrived, correctly dressed in Pakistani style—white pants, knee length black coat and black astrakhan cap. Naturally, he was bewildered over all the attention he was getting. He was small, but he stood up straight when Mr. Johnson greeted him. Soon they were on their way down to the LBJ Ranch.

He was given the royal tour of the ranch, including a ride out to the foothills, down to the ancestral home, and, of course, to the cemetery. There was a huge barbecue lunch for him with several guests, out on the lawn, and they finished the day with a motor boat ride on the lake. The next day Mr. Johnson took Bashir to the State Fair at Dallas where he and all of the guests were treated to a box lunch.

Mr. Johnson had also arranged for the camel driver to meet Mr. Kennedy, and Lady Bird brought him to the White House. We were extremely busy that day. All the rooms were taken for conferences and for that reason they had to wait in the hall. As Bashir and Lady Bird stood in front of my office waiting to go in to see Mr. Kennedy, I felt honestly sorry for him. He was playing the role of a diplomat and he was trying his best, but all of these strange people, who constantly stared at him, made him uneasy. Lady Bird, too, seemed impatient. She nervously swung her pocketbook back and forth. It seemed especially awkward because the only way you could talk to this ill-at-ease guest was through an interpreter, who was fidgety himself.

"The camel driver is here," I said to Mr. Kennedy as he came out of the Cabinet Room. "Fine, show him in," he replied. Just then the telephone rang. It was

Ambassador Stevenson. So while Mr. Kennedy was standing by my desk talking to the Ambassador I took Lady Bird and her guest into the oval office. Shortly, Mr. Kennedy joined them.

"Where's Lyndon?" I heard Mr. Kennedy say. "He's in Texas," Lady Bird answered. Mr. Kennedy then turned to the camel driver and as he did, the interpreter introduced them. With this, Mr. Kennedy held out his hand and told him how pleased he was to meet him. He asked him how he liked the United States, where he lived, and whether he had any children. The meeting was short, but it was pleasant. After a couple of pictures were taken of Mr. Kennedy, Lady Bird and the man from Pakistan, Mrs. Johnson ushered her guest through the door and out into the "fish room." It seemed to me an odd way for the Vice President of the United States to handle foreign relations.

Mr. Kennedy's trip to Europe the end of May was colorful and exciting, but his meeting with Khrushchev in Vienna was disappointing. After his return and during June and July there were rumblings out of West Berlin that the Russians were contemplating a new move. And that is exactly what they did. In the early part of August, they reinforced the wall between the two sectors of the city, and they closed all exits and entrances.

Mr. Kennedy was deeply concerned. The situation

looked grim and a trip to Europe might do some good. But he had just returned from Europe and felt that it was too early for him to go back. However, he felt it was important to send someone to reassure the people of West Berlin that we were back of them.

I heard my buzzer. "Mrs. Lincoln," he said, "will you get General Lucius Clay on the phone?" It took me quite a while to locate the General, but I finally did at 6:45 P.M. "Would you be willing to go to West Berlin?" I heard Mr. Kennedy ask the General. He must have said that he would be very glad to do anything that Mr. Kennedy desired because the rest of the conversation was made up of talk about the arrangements.

After he hung up the receiver the buzzer sounded once again. "Will you get Lyndon on the phone, Mrs. Lincoln?" At 7:15 P.M., he asked the same question of Mr. Johnson that he had asked General Clay. The response was completely different. The protests must have begun immediately, for I heard Mr. Kennedy say, "Yes, I know, but Lyndon . . ." Mr. Kennedy continued by saying, "But Lyndon, you are the logical man. We have to reassure the people in West Berlin and I wish you would do it." Then there was a long pause, while Mr. Kennedy listened to Mr. Johnson who must have been giving him more reasons why he thought he shouldn't go. However, Mr. Kennedy was insistent and said, "I have asked General Clay, and he has accepted. I was hoping that you would too."

Finally the Vice President did agree, and he and General Clay left for West Berlin on August 19th.

When Mr. Kennedy learned that Mr. Johnson had been urged by the Commander-in-chief, U.S. Army Forces in Europe, to remain in West Berlin to review the U.S. troops due to enter West Berlin on Sunday, August 20th, he said, "Oh, that's fine. Tell him to stay."

In the end Mr. Johnson was very helpful and Mr. Kennedy was extremely grateful to him for the manner in which he conducted himself there. He said so in his message to the press shortly after the Vice President's return.

He said, "The Vice President has given me an account of his remarkably successful visit to Germany and Berlin. His visit has made clear the extraordinary trust and confidence which the people of West Berlin place in our support for their freedom and the heavy responsibility that it places upon us. The situation in Berlin remains serious, and there will be much for all of us to do in support of freedom there in the months ahead. But I would like now to express my personal thanks to the Vice President, to General Clay and their associates for unusual service in this demonstration of the purpose of the United States."

The shocking news of the death of Dag Hammerskjold, the Secretary General to the United Nations, in an airplane crash over Africa saddened people all over the world. Mr. Kennedy once again turned to Mr. Johnson to serve as his representative at the funeral. This time Mr. Johnson did not object. "I would have liked to make this journey myself, and I am most grateful that you will act as the senior representative for the United States in my place," he told Mr. Johnson. As always, Kennedy gave Johnson other duties to perform on his trip. "On your way back you might stop off in Paris for discussions with Gavin, Finletter, and General Norstadt."

Mr. Kennedy gave Mr. Johnson a wonderful opportunity to study international problems first hand, because he assigned him to make more trips out of the country than any other Vice President in recent times. In 1962 the Vice President made two trips to Puerto Rico. The first was to attend the tenth anniversary of Puerto Rico as a commonwealth, and the other was as a good-will Ambassador.

When Mr. Kennedy asked him to attend the independence celebration in Jamaica, Mr. Johnson apparently accepted reluctantly. Before he left for Jamaica he called Walter Heller, Chairman of the Economic Advisors, and told him that he would not attend the economy meeting on August 9th. He told Mr. Heller that following his trip to Jamaica he was going directly to his ranch in Texas. Mr. Heller sensed that Mr. Johnson was upset so he asked me to tell Mr. Kennedy that he thought it would be a good idea for him to give Mr. Johnson a call down in Texas. When I told Mr. Kennedy what Mr. Heller had told me he said, "Why did he think I should call Lyndon?" I replied, "He didn't say so in so many words, but I think he feels that Mr. Johnson is hurt because you sent him off to Jamaica." Mr. Kennedy never replied, nor did he ever call Mr. Johnson about Jamaica.

Every trip was the same. Mr. Johnson didn't like the red tape surrounding a trip, and, most of all, he never liked to have anyone traveling with him who he thought might be spying on him. Mr. Kennedy always wanted someone who was with the State Department to accompany the Vice President to make sure that everything was in order and that all of the meetings and appointments were kept. Mr. Johnson was known to change plans at the last minute and then to get angry and upset if the officials in the various countries did not act promptly on the change of plans. Wherever he went it seemed as if he caused confusion.

Since the time the Soviets had sent Sputnik in orbit in 1957, Mr. Kennedy felt that it was important for the United States not only to catch up with them in this venture, but to surpass them. Shortly after his Inauguration the space race began.

Mr. Johnson, Chairman of the Space Council, was immediately pressed into action. In a memo he dictated to me, Mr. Kennedy asked Johnson to make an overall survey of where we stood in space. "Do we have a chance of beating the Soviets by putting a laboratory in space, or by a trip around the moon, or by a rocket to land on the moon, or by a rocket to go to the moon and back with a man? Is there any other space program which promises dramatic results in which we could win?" Then he wanted to know, "How much more will it cost? Are we making a maximum effort? Are we achieving necessary results?" And then he added, "Are we working 24 hours a day on existing programs? If not, why not? If not, will you make recommendations to me as to how work can be speeded up." He was asking Jim Webb, Dr. Jerome Wiesner, Secretary McNamara, and other officials to cooperate fully with the Vice President and he wanted "a report at the earliest possible moment."

Things were moving. On the 5th of May, Astronaut Shepard was about to be launched into space. I had my TV on, watching for the countdown. As Mr. Kennedy walked through my room on his way to the Cabinet Room for a meeting of the National Security Council he said, "Let me know just before the take-off." The countdown started. I rushed in to Mr. Kennedy. He followed me out of the office, as did Mr. Johnson and other members of the NSC. The take-off was electrifying.

Driving hard on his space program, Kennedy had further work for Mr. Johnson. This time he proposed that he conduct a study, at first hand, of the most important installations participating in the space program. He said in another memo to him, "In your visits to space installations, I hope you will give particular attention to the objective of attaining the highest possible level of effectivness in making use of the scientific and technological talent available to this program."

Colonel John H. Glenn was set to be launched into outer space, but there was difficulty getting him off the pad. Eight times they postponed his flight. Then on February 20th he made it, circled the earth three times, and landed successfully. Mr. Kennedy was extremely pleased and when he talked to Colonel Glenn aboard the U.S.S. *Noa,* he said to him, "I am coming down to Canaveral on Friday, and hope you will come up to Washington on Monday and Tuesday, and we will be looking forward to seeing you there."

When Mr. Johnson learned that Mr. Kennedy was going to Cape Canaveral to see Colonel Glenn on Friday, he could not contain himself. He suddenly realized what effect this was going to have on the people of the United States, and, as chairman of the space committee, he wanted to get credit for it. Once again his immediate thought was of his image. Although Mr. Kennedy invited him to come to Cape Canaveral, Mr. Johnson didn't want to do it that way. He wanted to go to the Grand Turk Island in the Bahamas, where Colonel Glenn was going to stay and then fly *with* Colonel Glenn to Cape Canaveral to meet Mr. Kennedy. No amount of persuasion could sway him. Mr. Kennedy said, "This is Colonel Glenn's triumph and Lyndon should realize that."

The greatest protests came when he insisted on

riding down Broadway with Colonel Glenn through the ticker tape and confetti. He made such a fuss that Mr. Kennedy finally consented.

Cartoons often have a way of portraying, in a humorous but searching way, how events appear to the man in the street, and there was one during this time that did just that. It showed Colonel Glenn slumped down in a chair mopping his brow. His wife was standing right by him saying, "They've all left, dear. The photographers, Lyndon Johnson . . ."

Mr. Kennedy was not content to rely upon written reports concerning the space centers. He was anxious to see for himself what they were doing, so plans were being made to visit four space centers. Mr. Johnson was included in the planning.

As they were working on the plans for this trip Mr. Johnson insisted on riding with Mr. Kennedy on Air Force One. Once again, he knew there would be crowds. Once again, he was thinking of his image. "You don't mean to tell me that Mr. Johnson is making that same request to ride on Air Force One with me on our way to Huntsville?" Mr. Kennedy asked. "Can't we ever get it through his head that it can't be done because of security reasons?"

They were in separate planes when we took off the morning of the 11th of September, but what a struggle it was to accomplish this.

Our first stop on this trip was Redstone Army Airfield, Huntsville, Alabama, where we were greeted by

Dr. Wernher von Braun, Director of the Marshall Space Flight Center. He and his associates took us through many displays of Guidance Control Equipment and briefed us on the advanced Saturn Rocket.

From Huntsville we flew to Cape Canaveral, and, from there, to the Houston, Texas International Airport. It was right at a time when the traffic on the streets was at its height. The streets were lined and the windows were packed as we wormed our way into the city and on to the Rice Hotel. This had been a big day, and I was glad that this was our last stop. However, we had to get up early because Mr. Kennedy was going to speak at Rice University.

The stadium was packed the next morning, as he told them how much the space program would mean to Texas, to the West, and to the nation.

This trip generated a feeling of appreciation among the people who worked in those space centers, and it pleased Mr. Kennedy very much to see first hand the great strides in the race into outer space that had been made since 1961.

Mr. Johnson was also Chairman of the President's Committee on Equal Employment Opportunity. That committee from the very beginning had been plagued with friction and bickering. Jerry R. Holleman, Assistant Secretary of Labor, who worked with the committee, was from Texas and when it was learned that he had connections with Billie Sol Estes, another Texan, and had accepted money from him for personal expenses, Mr. Kennedy permitted him to resign.

Then Mr. Johnson objected to committee staff member Mr. Robert Troutman of Atlanta, Georgia. He felt that Troutman was taking too much on himself on a committee of which Mr. Johnson was the official head. "Bob" was deeply devoted to the Kennedy family because of his friendship with Mr. Kennedy's older brother, Joe, Jr. He and other staff members started a program which they called "Plans for Progress" whereby they would contact businessmen and interest them in participating. They were very successful. The first signing of businessmen took place on November 30, 1961, and the second signing was held in the State Dining Room of the White House in the presence of Mr. Kennedy and Mr. Johnson. There were nineteen businesses represented. Bob worked hard on this program, but in the end, he resigned.

Sometimes Mr. Johnson was brought into negotiations and other times he wasn't. Mr. Johnson himself would, from time to time, mention a meeting he had learned was scheduled, and ask to be included. He would receive an invitation and then, for one or two meetings more, would be on the list of participants.

Then, his name would be dropped and various meetings would take place without him present. I never heard anyone say, "Let's exclude Lyndon," but the fact is that his name appeared less and less on the lists of those who were invited to crucial White House policy and planning meetings. As a matter of fact, he was around the White House office a lot less by this time, than he had been at the beginning of the Administration. At the time Roger Blough blew the lid off of the steel prices, Mr. Johnson didn't find out about it until he came to the White House to attend the congressional reception at 9:30 P.M. that evening. He was asked to attend a breakfast meeting the next morning to discuss the situation, but during all of the other meetings, Mr. Johnson was not consulted. There is no doubt that he offered to help and perhaps did contact some of his friends but Charley Bartlett, Clark Clifford, and Secretary Goldberg, together with other Kennedy contacts, were able to persuade U.S. Steel and other companies to rescind the price hike.

The dropping of Mr. Johnson from various meetings had been very gradual, but it was no doubt noticeable to Johnson's followers. As early as May 9, 1962, they were beginning to wonder how Mr. Kennedy felt about Mr. Johnson. At his press conference on that day, a newsman hopped up and said to Mr. Kennedy, "Mr. President, there have been rumors in print, in and out of Texas, that Vice President Johnson might be dropped from the Democratic ticket in 1964. I'd like to ask if you have any reason whatever to believe that either end of the Democratic ticket will be different in 1964?" Mr. Kennedy answered in the only way he could. This was 1962, and the election was two years away.

He said: "Well, I don't know what they will do

with me, but I am sure that the Vice President will be on the ticket if he chooses to run. We were fortunate to have him before—and would be again—and I don't know where such a rumor would start. He's invaluable. He fulfills a great many responsibilities as Vice President. He participates in all the major deliberations. He's been in the Congress for years. He is invaluable. So, of course, he will be, if he chooses to be, part of the ticket."

Then, came the long, tense packed moments during the Cuban Crisis in October 1962.

At that time my office became the meeting place for many of those about to go into the conferences that were being held in the Cabinet Room. I heard so many discussions, so many arguments, that sometimes I wondered if the whole Cuban Crisis was going to be decided right in front of my desk. In addition, all top secret mail was shuttled through my hands to Mr. Kennedy.

Mr. Johnson was at all the briefings, meetings, and participated in the important decisions. He was chiefly concerned with what was taking place in Cuba and entered the discussions the same as all of the other participants. However, after all of the discussions, all of the briefings, all of the arguments, it was up to Mr. Kennedy to make the decision as to what was to be done. I will never forget the moment he came out of the Cabinet Room after the decision had been made and said, "That's it, if somebody doesn't foul it up." It wasn't fouled up, and he certainly won that battle.

Even though Mr. Kennedy had always been the man in charge, from the day that Khrushchev agreed to pull out the missiles, the President had an added ingredient of self-confidence. It seemed as though he had turned the corner and was now going up a different street. He relied more on his own staff and advisors than on the politicians. After the Cuban Crisis, Mr. Kennedy seemed to be less concerned with making sure the Vice President was occupied and, from then on, he let Mr. Johnson seek his own place in the administration.

The elections in November turned out well, too. In off-year elections, the party out of power usually picks up from 25 to 35 new seats in the House. But this year all they picked up were 4.

The tenseness and worry that had existed since way before the Inauguration had finally been lifted and 1963, at that time, was really welcome. Even his State of the Union message to the joint session of Congress was reassuring. "My friends," he said, "I close on a note of hope. We are not lulled by the momentary calm on the sea or the somewhat clearer skies above. We know the turbulence that lies below, and the storms that are beyond the horizon this year. But now the winds of change appear to be blowing more strongly than ever, in the world of communism as well as our own. For 175 years we have sailed with those winds at our back, and with the tides of human freedom in our favor. We steer our ship with hope, as Thomas Jefferson said, 'leaving fear astern.'

"Today we still welcome those winds of change—and we have every reason to believe that our tide is running strong. With thanks to Almighty God for seeing us through a perilous passage, we ask His help anew in guiding the 'Good Ship Union.' "

By his actions it seemed as though Mr. Johnson was becoming more and more aware of Mr. Kennedy's changed attitude toward the office of the Presidency. In fact, as Mr. Kennedy's sureness and independence increased, the Vice President became more apprehensive and anxious to please. He tried even harder to enter into activities and become a part of them.

What was noticeable to me was how Mr. Johnson often was looking for opportunities to praise Mr. Kennedy. Whenever anyone mentioned Mr. Kennedy's name he would immediately tell them what a good job he was doing. He praised the efficiency of the Kennedy staff and the soundness of the Kennedy ideas. Time and time again, as they filed out of the Cabinet Room, I would hear Mr. Johnson making these glowing compliments. Mr. Kennedy talked for 45 minutes at a meeting of the National Security Council at 11:00 A.M. on January 22nd telling them the objectives for the coming months. Mr. Johnson elbowed his way through the group standing in my room after the meeting until he came up to the President. He stuck out his hand and said, "That was a fine speech, Jack."

He even tried to make it appear that all was well with him in his own job. On March 26, 1963 when he was discussing his duties with three reporters, he said, "President Kennedy and the members of his staff and Cabinet have given me every opportunity to be aware of all the important decisions that have been made and to participate in them, and to make any recommendations I care to make." This was quite a bit different than the stories he put out in 1961 when he said that he just sat in the meetings and listened.

When he returned from a trip to the Dominican Republic, Mr. Johnson sent a letter to Mr. Kennedy telling him what a wonderful job the Secret Service had done for him during this trip. This was a change in attitude since Mr. Johnson did not usually like them to restrict his activities. He commented that the alertness, efficiency, imagination, and intelligence of the Secret Service detail kept the one known attempt at a demonstration from becoming a national incident. He said that they worked so smoothly that he was even able to get out of his car to shake hands with the people. Mr. Johnson was his old self in the Dominican Republic, jumping in and out of the cars shaking hands, but this time he praised the efforts of the Secret Service.

Mr. Kennedy was grateful to Mr. Johnson for representing him at the inauguration of Juan Bosch as

President of the Dominican Republic. It may have seemed like a thankless task to him. Ambassador Martin wrote concerning Johnson's visit, "I had heard that he was difficult and that other ambassadors dreaded his visits. I did not find him so."

But one Latin American diplomat remarked, "If there's anything which puts our teeth on edge it's a Texan who speaks a little Spanish." The unfortunate Vice President was being saddled with a lot of unhappy history along the Rio Grande.

Even Juan Bosch, the man Mr. Johnson had come to honor, had his mind on Mr. Kennedy and not on his representative. Mr. Johnson did little to inspire confidence in Bosch because later after Kennedy's death the former Dominican President stated in his memoirs, ". . . although the machinery of this Alliance for Progress survived him, the vitality and spirit of reform with which he imbued it died with him in Dallas . . . and so I write about the Alliance for Progress in the past tense."

The President was prodding Mr. Johnson less now, sending him fewer memos and giving him fewer assignments, and, as a result, Johnson was fading into the background. Once in a while Mr. Kennedy would stop by my desk and say, "Be sure that Johnson is advised of the civil rights meeting tomorrow," or "Let Johnson know that the off-record meeting has been postponed."

I hate to admit it, but in planning the surprise

birthday party for Mr. Kennedy on May 29th, I forgot all about inviting Mr. Johnson. And no one reminded me.

Mr. Johnson might have been calm and submissive down around the White House, but up in the Capitol he was a tyrant. My father-in-law came home night after night with tales of what Mr. Johnson had said in the reception room. Dad Lincoln would say to me, "What did you do to Mr. Johnson down there in the White House today? He was so mad and he swore so much that people were relieved when he went into his office and banged the door after him."

Another time he came home and said that Mr. Johnson stood right in front of his desk waving his arms and shouting, "I'd like to get out of this damn town, go back to Texas and never come back." His secretary came to work one day and found that her parking place had been taken. That also happened to another secretary of his, Mary Margaret Wiley (now Mrs. Valenti). Both times he steamed out of his office looking for the young culprit who was responsible for letting someone park in that parking place. He cursed at everyone all along the line until he found what he thought was the right one, and then he really went to town with his strong language. My father-in-law, who started to work in that reception room in 1961, said Mr. Johnson rarely had a kind word to say to anyone.

Mr. Johnson was showing his anxiety in other ways.

He became quite upset by some remarks that appeared in the *New York Times,* accredited to Congressman James Roosevelt before the General Subcommittee on Labor. Mr. Johnson thought that the Congressman was criticizing him personally, but as it turned out, Roosevelt was not criticizing Mr. Johnson or the members of the Committee on Equal Employment Opportunity. What he was trying to say was that he thought the committee needed more resources to give it the ability to properly police existing agreements.

Many members of Congress wanted Mr. Johnson to come to their districts or states to make speeches for them, but he turned most of them down. Some of them called me. They wanted me to ask Mr. Kennedy if he could ask Johnson to accept. Several times Mr. Kennedy asked me to call the Vice President and find out if he could make it and, although he said he would look into it, generally Liz Carpenter would call me and tell me that he had another commitment on that day. Perhaps with all the official international travel he was doing, Mr. Johnson did not wish to be away from Washington any further time.

One day Senator Dirksen called on Mr. Kennedy. After he left, Mr. Kennedy came out to my desk and said, "Do you know what the Senator told me today? Dirksen told me, 'Let's face it, Eisenhower did not know much about what was going on during his Administration. He would call a group in—let the others do most of the talking—he used to sit and doodle for about two hours and then he would say, "Okay, boys, who is going to carry the ball?"' The Senator said that it was frightening—Eisenhower's lack of knowledge of what was taking place and the things he didn't know about the United States Government. Nixon used to call on Dirksen and ask him to speak to Eisenhower, particularly about firing Sherman Adams. But the Senator said that he told Nixon he should talk to Eisenhower, he was the Vice President, but Nixon was scared of Eisenhower."

"Well," I said to Mr. Kennedy, "you and Mr. Johnson are certainly different than those two men. You certainly know what you are doing and Mr. Johnson is not afraid of you." "No," said Mr. Kennedy, "the only thing Mr. Johnson is afraid of is that I will not put him on the ticket in 1964."

CHAPTER

XII

Growing Unrest

IN OCTOBER 1963 there were two storms brewing that could easily engulf Mr. Johnson. One was the Bobby Baker scandal, and the other was the vicious political battle going on among all of the Democratic factions in Texas.

The first, the Bobby Baker case, came to light in September 1963 when a vending company filed a suit against Baker for not fulfilling a contract.

The news and the reports that were filtering in about Bobby and his transactions were disturbing to the occupants of the White House for two reasons. First, Bobby Baker had used his connections to help swing doubtful business deals his way. Although he was no longer on Mr. Johnson's staff, he had a way of beginning a business conversation with, "Well, Lyndon told me the other day."

If you worked for a United States Senator, Democratic or Republican you knew Bobby Baker, Secretary to the Majority. His relationship with Mr. Johnson, then Majority Leader, was extremely close, so close that during the campaign in Dixie in 1960 Mr. Johnson asked him to take charge of his "Corn Ball Express."

As they criss-crossed the South they came into South Carolina, very close to Pickens, Baker's hometown. At that stop they got off the train, piled into a helicopter and flew to Pickens to do a little hand shakin' with home folks. With his arm around Bobby, Mr. Johnson said to them, "Bobby is my strong right arm. He is the last person I see at night and the first person I see in the morning."

Mr. Kennedy's high standards were now rubbing against the ragged surface of the Bobby Baker case. There were bound to be sparks—and they would fly, fairly or unfairly, at Mr. Johnson.

Senator John Williams, a Republican from Deleware, became interested in the case and started to do some investigating on his own. (Much, much later came the report about "Johnson warning the Republicans via the grapevine that if they press him too hard on Bobby Baker, some G.O.P. tax returns will be audited.") At the same time, the Department of Justice started an investigation. They both dug in more deeply. Pressures were mounting: Bobby Baker was in trouble and, October 7, 1963, he resigned.

What was Mr. Kennedy's reaction to all of this?

Mr. Kennedy had always insisted upon honesty in

government. This is one of the many reasons why I volunteered to work for him in 1952. As early as October 1960 he had stated clearly in the Washington newspapers what his views were on the conduct of the members of the Executive Branch. These principles, he said, were:

"An official in the Government of the United States must have one allegiance, and one allegiance only—a complete dedication to the interests of the National Government. He must never be allowed to have other interests which might conflict with that overriding principle.

"First," Kennedy said, "the office holder must exercise great judgment in selecting men who will be faithful to these principles. He must make clear, through appropriate regulations, the exact points at which public interests and private interest conflict.

"Next, he must act immediately to remove from his Administration any who violate the principles and regulations he has laid down."

Mr. Kennedy kept a close tab on his own aides. He watched that they did not become lax in their standards. When one did—like a flash he was out of the Administration. No matter how busy or preoccupied Kennedy was, he was always kept informed about such infractions. He never believed a high government official could afford the excuse that he "wasn't aware of what was going on." Such lame excuses made him very angry at those who used them and he wouldn't permit himself to do what he deplored in others.

The Senate Rules Committee, which had now decided to investigate Baker's financial and political career, announced that hearings would begin on October 30th. As he made the announcement Chairman B. Everett Jordan of North Carolina said, "We are starting with the Bobby Baker case. Where it spreads from there we don't know."

Mr. Kennedy, in his press conference on November 14, 1963, was asked about criticism of the moral and ethical climate generally, and about the Bobby Baker scandal specifically. He replied that there were people in all professions, including government, "who can't stand the pressure of opportunity." In reviewing the record, he said, "I think that this Administration has been very vigorous in its action and I think we have tried to set a responsible standard. There are always going to be people who fail to meet that standard, and we attempt to take appropriate action dealing with each case."

Then, he added, "But Mr. Baker is now being investigated, and I think we will have a good deal more about Mr. Baker before we are through. Other people may be investigated as time goes on. We just try to do the best we can."

There was a second storm brewing around Mr. Johnson with its center in Texas politics and that was the smoldering feud going on between Governor

John B. Connally, a conservative, Senator Ralph W. Yarborough, a liberal, and Mr. Johnson. Senator John Tower, a conservative Republican who had taken Mr. Johnson's seat in the Senate, was doing his best to keep from being dragged into the holocaust.

The bone of contention among all of the contenders was the persistent rumor that Mr. Johnson would not be on the ticket in 1964. The Bobby Baker scandal was not helping to squelch that rumor. Neither was Mr. Johnson. I was told by my father-in-law that time after time Johnson would storm out of his office into the reception room and shout to someone walking with him, "Why does the White House always have it in for me? I'm going back to Texas and run for the United States Senate against Senator Yarborough."

There is no doubt that President Kennedy hoped Mr. Johnson would publicly disavow Baker and that Johnson would have preferred to let the whole thing blow over. Any White House pressure would have rankled the Vice President.

Governor John B. Connally was uneasy, and he was also ambitious. He was thinking of his own political future—perhaps he would like to run for the Senate some day, like to be Vice President, and who knows, maybe the President. Some of his conservative supporters were saying that Mr. Johnson was a liberal sell-out to Mr. Kennedy. Therefore, because of his public connection with Mr. Johnson, he was very anxious for Mr. Johnson to be on the national ticket and not come back to Texas and muddy the waters for him. Connally came to Washington to see Mr. Kennedy just three days before Bobby Baker resigned. His main purpose was to urge the President to come down to Texas to help bring the feuding factions together.

After he left I remember what Mr. Kennedy said: "He sure seemed anxious for me to go to Texas. He attracts some people—money people who would never vote for me, but I have many supporters down there who are bitterly opposed to him. I think in the long run it would be more advantageous to him than for me. The one thing I noticed above everything else was his concern about Lyndon being on the ticket."

Senator Ralph W. Yarborough, too, was definitely opposed to having Mr. Johnson come back to Texas and run against him, and he was doing everything possible to prevent it. His friends and supporters planned an appreciation—a statewide Texas Salute dinner for him in Austin, on October 19th. A very imposing list of Senators and Congressmen had accepted the invitation to show their support of Yarborough. They were to be seated at the head table and were to make short speeches. Included among them were Senators Olin D. Johnston of South Carolina, Lee Metcalf of Montana, Ernest Gruening of Alaska, Daniel K. Inouye of Hawaii, Frank Church of Idaho, and Congressmen Jack Brooks and Henry Gonzalez of Texas. Postmaster General John A. Gronouski was the principal speaker. To top it all, there was a message on film by Mr. Kennedy. Mr. Johnson was conspicuous by his absence.

The program, which was to be distributed during the dinner, contained statements concerning the Senator's accomplishments. These complimentary messages were from Senator Mike Mansfield, Senator Hubert Humphrey, Senator Warren G. Magnuson, Senator Lister Hill, Senator Paul Douglas, Senator Ted Kennedy, Senator John Sparkman, Senator Philip A. Hart, and Austin's Mayor, Lester B. Palmer. Senator Yarborough wanted to make sure that everyone in the White House knew how much support he had from his colleagues in the Congress and what a mistake it would be for anyone else to run. Shortly after this unusually star-studded dinner, the Senator came personally to my office with autographed copies of the program to be distributed to the various Kennedy staff members. I told him that I would be delighted to see that they were distributed—and this is exactly what I did.

Every time a new development was uncovered in the Bobby Baker case, the "drop Lyndon" rumors would begin again and each time they grew louder and louder. At the height of all of these rumors, in the latter part of October, Mr. Johnson left Washington for a visit to his ranch in Texas.

Reluctantly, Mr. Kennedy agreed to go to Texas. Advance reports from our own staff and from many other people gave us cause to worry about the tense climate in Texas—and, most especially, in Dallas. Dallas was removed and then put back on the planned itinerary several times. Our own advance man urged that the motorcade not take the route through the underpass and past the Book Depository, but he was overruled.

There were long discussions about who would sit in what car in the motorcade, and most of all, Texas political maneuvering did not seem to want Senator Yarborough to sit anywhere.

In later years, Governor Connally and others in Texas have incorrectly maintained that Mr. Kennedy came to Texas not to settle political feuds there, but to save his own sinking political popularity. For this reason, it is important to stress that there was a center of quiet confidence in the Kennedy political camp at that time, unaffected by the breaking storm of Bobby Baker in Washington and the factional quarreling in Johnson's home state. These matters had bearing on Mr. Johnson's political popularity, not on the President's.

On November 12, nine days before his trip to Texas, Mr. Kennedy held a political strategy session in the Cabinet Room to plan the 1964 campaign. The meeting included most of the Kennedy top political strategists, including his brother Bob, John Bailey, Ted Sorensen, Steve Smith, Larry O'Brien, Kenny O'Donnell, and others. It should be noted that interestingly enough, the meeting did not include Mr. Johnson. This strategy meeting lasted from 4:00 o'clock in the afternoon into the evening and was off the record.

However, the material they had discussed passed over my desk the following morning. I noticed that they had taken up such subjects as the convention program, registration, regional coordinators, and the speakers bureau. As I was reading, Mr. Kennedy stopped by my desk. I said to him, "There will never be another convention like the one in 1960. This one will not be as exciting because everyone knows what is coming."

"Oh, I don't know, there might be a change in the ticket," he said to me, as he walked on into the Cabinet Room.

I thought then, that there was something real in the rumors I had been hearing. The strategy meeting also analyzed Kennedy's prospects, as shown in major national polls, as well as in regional and state polls.

It seemed likely, at that time, that Mr. Kennedy would be running against Senator Goldwater. The polls showed him running far ahead of Goldwater and it looked as if he might well be on his way to the kind of victory which would give him the power to complete the process of getting his legislative program through Congress. Surprising enough, the polls showed him running better against Nixon than he was against Goldwater. The respected Beldon poll of Texas showed him running slightly ahead of Goldwater even in Texas, which was said to be a second home for the Arizona Senator.

Much has been said about Mr. Kennedy's popularity at this time, but these figures indicate his standing in the polls which he had before him, shortly before his trip to Texas. This good news was reinforced by a trip to Florida a few days later, where the warmth of the crowds gave evidence of his popularity even in the South.

CHAPTER XIII

A Decision That Was Not Fulfilled

THIS DAY, November 19, 1963, started like any other day. There was the usual ride down 16th Street, past the guard at the Northwest Gate, who waved to me as we went by, into the reception room, the exchanging of greetings with the guard at the door, the long walk down the hallway, and then into my office. We had returned the night before from a trip to New York City, Tampa, Palm Beach, and Miami, so my desk was piled high with unanswered mail and there were bags and boxes of accumulated letters, telegrams, speeches, and gifts from the trip lying on the floor near the wall.

I busied myself with my usual duties of checking Mr. Kennedy's desk and office to make sure that everything was in readiness for him when he came over from the Mansion.

Then came his usual call. "When is my first appointment, Mrs. Lincoln?" "At ten," I replied, "with the Poultry and Egg National Board and Senator Dirksen. They are bringing you a turkey for Thanksgiving." "Oh yes, that's right. All right, I'll be over in a little while."

When he came over at about 9:25, the first thing he wanted to know was, "Where are Kenny O'Donnell and Dave Powers?" When I told him that they were worn out from the trip and would not be in, he remarked, "We were on that trip too, but we are here, aren't we, Mrs. Lincoln?" He was right, there was no doubt about that.

As I look back on this day I remember it as one of the most pleasant days I ever spent with Mr. Kennedy in the White House.

There was no hurry, no tension, no hustle and no bustle. Although he saw many people, he would sit in my office for as long as a half an hour at a time discussing various issues and situations. Mr. Kennedy had returned from a trip which included a relaxing weekend in Palm Beach where he said as he rode to the airport with his old friend Congressman Torbert Macdonald, "This was really living. I will never forget it."

Between appointments, we discussed the trip to New York and the relaxation of police protection. Mr. Kennedy was impressed with his trip to Florida and the realization that he had support on his own, not merely in Florida, but in several other southern states. Another time we talked about the pictures that

Stan Tretick of *Look* magazine took of John and of how John had grown. Mr. Kennedy loved having John and Caroline near his office at the White House. He liked the people to see them, like the proud father he was—and almost exclusive of whatever "political" asset they might be.

Then, we discussed civil rights and the mounting tension in the cities. We discussed the Bobby Baker case and the effects of this scandal on the campaign. And then we came to the trip to Texas and Mr. Johnson.

As Mr. Kennedy sat in the rocker in my office, his head resting on its back he placed his left leg across his right knee. He rocked slightly as he talked. In a slow pensive voice he said to me, "You know if I am reelected in sixty-four, I am going to spend more and more time toward making government service an honorable career. I would like to tailor the executive and legislative branches of government so that they can keep up with the tremendous strides and progress being made in other fields. We are no longer in the horse and buggy age—nor the speeding car age—we are now in the space age, and it is most unfortunate that bills can be tied up in a committee by a man who, because of his longevity, is the chairman. Therefore, I am going to advocate changing some of the outmoded rules and regulations in the Congress, such as the seniority rule.

"To do this I will need as a running mate in sixty-four a man who believes as I do. I am going to Texas, because I have made a commitment. I can't patch up those warring factions. This is for them to do, but I will go because I have told them I would. And it is too early to make an announcement about another running-mate—that will perhaps wait until the convention."

I was fascinated by this conversation and wrote it down verbatim in my diary. I was extremely proud of the man with whom I was associated. I was also glad that I could be a part of the goals and ambitions he was striving for in the future.

He had talked and I had just listened, but I did venture one question. We had not seen Mr. Johnson since he left for Texas in late October. Now I asked, "Who is your choice as a running-mate?"

He looked straight ahead, and without hesitating he replied, "At this time I am thinking about Governor Terry Sanford of North Carolina. But it will not be Lyndon."

This news was not shocking to me. It had been my feeling for quite a while that Lyndon Johnson would not be the Vice-Presidential candidate in the next campaign. In fact, I had discussed this possibility with my husband and friends many times. I related to them the interest with which President Kennedy had followed the work of Governor Terry Sanford. He, of course, had welcomed Sanford's counsel and help at the Los Angeles convention, during the southern meetings of the rump session in Congress, and on the campaign trail in North Carolina. Both Mr. Kennedy and Mr. Sanford believed it was what you do with political effort which counts and Mr. Kennedy had watched with interest Mr. Sanford's efforts to tackle some of his state's problems of poverty and of economic growth. Some of Mr. Sanford's efforts were incorporated into the federal programs concerning poverty.

In his Inaugural Address at Raleigh, on January 5, 1961, Governor Sanford pledged himself to a program of educational progress and economic development. He told the assembled guests, who saw him take office as North Carolina's ninety-third governor, that he wanted the state to move into "the mainstream of American life." The *New York Times* in an editorial on January 15, 1961, praised Sanford for measuring North Carolina's future on the national scale rather than in comparison with other states below the Mason-Dixon line.

In line with his policy of cooperating with the Kennedy Administration, Governor Sanford urged North Carolina Congressmen, late in January 1961, to support the Administration's proposals to liberalize the House Rules Committee, in order to avert the obstruction of a large part of the President's legislative program.

Mr. Sanford attended the White House meeting on the poverty of the Appalachians and he headed one of the most attractive teams working on that problem. He brought some of his planning directors and other assistants with him. Everyone was impressed with the imagination and determination they showed in attacking the problems of economic development in their areas.

Mr. Kennedy discussed other things as the day went along—but it was a day to remember.

I tucked these thoughts, along with many others, in the back of my mind. There was work to do—bags to pack, and a hundred and one things to put away until we came back.

We flew off to Texas a couple of days later.

We returned from Dallas on Air Force One on November 22nd. I came back to my office for a few minutes at 8:00 the very next morning, but he never returned to his.

My things—all of Mr. Kennedy's things—would have to be removed.

About the Author

Evelyn Lincoln is the daughter of the late Congressman, J. N. Norton of Nebraska. She has a B.A. from George Washington University, where she also studied law for two years. She is married to political scientist, Harold Lincoln, and lives with him in Bethesda, Maryland. Mrs. Lincoln has been associated with the office of the Majority Clerk of the House of Representatives, with Congressman Forrester of Georgia, and, of course, spent twelve years as personal secretary to John F. Kennedy. She has worked extensively on the Kennedy papers, which will eventually be included in the John F. Kennedy Library in Cambridge.

21 DAY BOOK

NEW HANOVER COUNTY PUBLIC LIBRARY
3 4200 00169 7701

320.973
L
Lincoln, Evelyn
Kennedy and Johnson.
DISCARDED
from
New Hanover County Public Library
Wilmington Public Library
Wilmington, N. C. 28401